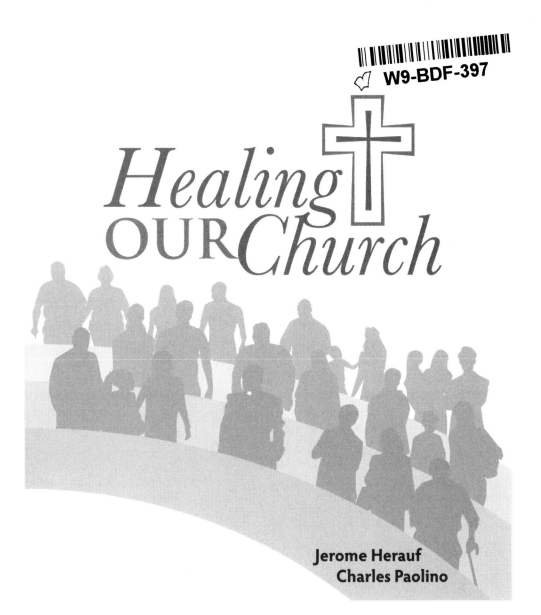

Healing ✝ OUR *Church*

Jerome Herauf
Charles Paolino

RENEW
INTERNATIONAL

Unless otherwise noted, scripture passages are from the New Revised Standard Version Bible: Catholic Edition, © 1989, 1993 the Division of Christian Education of the National Council of the Churches of Christ in the United States of America. Used by permission. All rights reserved.

FAITH-SHARING SESSIONS:

NIHIL OBSTAT
Rev. Lawrence Porter, Ph.D., S.T.L., S.T.B.

IMPRIMATUR
Joseph W. Cardinal Tobin, C.Ss.R.
Archbishop of Newark

Cover and interior design by Ruth Markworth

ISBN: 978-1-62063-149-2

RENEW International
1232 George Street
Plainfield, NJ 07062-1717
www.renewintl.org

RENEW International is a 501 (c)(3) non-profit organization.

Printed and bound in the United States of America

FOREWORD

The Pennsylvania grand-jury report in the summer of 2018 and the allegations against former Cardinal McCarrick reopened the wounds of the clergy sexual-abuse crisis and coverup. As I read the detail of the crimes committed against the most vulnerable, I experienced anger, disillusionment, and shame. I wanted to distance myself from it all. As I began to listen to the anger and pain of everyday Catholics while facilitating parish listening sessions, buying groceries in the neighborhood, and attending family gatherings, I knew I had to do something. As I worked through my anger, the Holy Spirit slowly brought me to the truth that I needed to be part of reforming and rebuilding the Church—this Church that I love and that formed me in my faith. I needed to act for the sake of the majority of the faithful lay women and men, clergy, and religious who follow the way of Jesus—these faith-filled Catholics who celebrate the sacraments, pray daily, and are committed to charitable works and just acts. My co-workers at RENEW felt the same way. We needed to do our part to heal OUR Church.

A quote from theologian Karl Rahner inspires me: "I acknowledge that the Church has caused me much grief, but it is a heaviness I am not willing to put down. I will carry it until it is transformed into life, and the burden becomes light."

We at RENEW recommit ourselves "to carry the Church until it is transformed into life." With this in our hearts and minds, we developed *Healing Our Church* primarily for "people in the pews"—to face the truth, rebuild the Church, and find a way forward together as a family of faith. *Healing Our Church* is a small-group process that includes prayer, stories of victim-survivors, reflections on Scripture and the sexual-abuse crisis, and faith sharing—all leading to action. The suggested action steps are small and doable and are directed mostly at the local level where effective global action often begins.

This small-group resource has been a work of love and a myriad of people have worked unceasingly over the last months to get it ready for Lent 2019. I am grateful to Charles Paolino, co-author and editor, and co-author Jerry Herauf. They were aided by an advisory committee made up of health professionals, professional ministers, and dedicated lay people: Alice Brown; Fr. John Collins, C.Ss.R.; Dr. Thomas Plante; Sr. Honora Nicholson, RSM; Sr. Janet Schaeffler, OP; Sr. Donna Ciangio, OP, and Msgr. Richard Arnhols. I am grateful to Bishop Alfred Schlert of the Diocese of Allentown, Pennsylvania, for pushing us to get this done because he felt strongly, "My people need healing now." I am grateful to all my colleagues at RENEW who put aside other projects to contribute to developing and implementing this resource.

I am convinced the treatment needed to heal our wounded Church is truth, compassion, transparency, accountability, and prayer. And it will take all of us—empowered lay women and men, priests, deacons, religious, and bishops, working together, to heal and transform our Church.

Sr. Theresa Rickard, OP, DMin
President and Executive Director
RENEW International

TABLE OF CONTENTS

ABOUT THE AUTHORS

Jerome Herauf was senior editor with Novalis Publishers for fifteen years, responsible for a variety of pastoral materials, and notably editor of the *Living with Christ* missalette. Following his departure from Novalis, he has contracted widely as a freelance writer with several national Catholic and Christian organizations. More recently, he worked with **RENEW** International in developing and maintaining the **RENEW** website through writing and project and editing management.

Charles Paolino is managing editor at RENEW International. He is a columnist for the *Catholic Spirit*, the newspaper of the Diocese of Metuchen, and the author of several books of Lenten and Advent reflections in *The Living Gospel* series by Ave Maria Press. He is a permanent deacon of the Diocese of Metuchen.

A NOTE ABOUT THE MUSIC

Songs are suggested for the moments of prayer at the opening of each session of this book. Music selections for *Healing Our Church* are provided by our partners at OCP. The music is available as individual songs or as a six-song digital album or "virtual CD." The individual songs and the digital album are available for purchase through RENEW International at ocp.org/renew-music.

INTRODUCTION

The Roman Catholic Church in the United States and in many other parts of the world has experienced a seismic quake with the revelation of sexual abuse of minor children and teens perpetrated by Catholic priests over many decades. The sexual victimization of youth by Catholic priests is horrific enough, but the coverups by high-ranking clerics including bishops and cardinals in many locations has added terrible aftershocks to the story.

In the United States, reports of sexual abuse by priests began to appear in the press as early as the 1980s, but it wasn't until January 6, 2002 that the dots were connected, and the *Boston Globe's* Spotlight team published a front-page report about abuse and coverup in the Archdiocese of Boston that galvanized the attention of Catholics and non-Catholics alike. After over a decade of crisis, the Academy of Motion Pictures Arts and Sciences gave the film, *Spotlight* (based on the *Boston Globe's* groundbreaking reporting), the academy's highest honor, the Oscar, as best picture of the year in 2015. And just when it seemed that the Church had put this terrible story behind it, another crisis unfolded with the release of the Pennsylvania Grand Jury Report during the summer of 2018, detailing 70 years of clergy sexual abuse in that state, followed by other state grand-jury reports and decisions by dioceses and religious orders to release the names of all clerics credibly accused of sexual victimization of minors over many decades, and further reports of high-ranking clerics, including bishops and cardinals, sexually violating seminarians in the Church as well.

Sadly and tragically, even with so much attention focused on the problem of clerical sexual abuse and coverups in the Catholic Church, it is very challenging to get quality and reliable information on the facts surrounding the crisis. Many have tried to use the scandal to serve their own political and other agendas. Those who tend to be most conservative want to blame the problem on homosexual priests or on the changes in the Church associated with Vatican II. Those who lean on the liberal side tend to blame the problem on celibacy or the lack of women in leadership positions in the Church, including as clerics. And those who tend toward anti-Catholic bias and bigotry are rather pleased if not delighted to blame the problem on the Church as a whole, wishing to see it collapse and die.

In the meantime, many people are deeply impacted by the abuse and its aftermath. First and foremost are the victims who have suffered not only from sexual abuse at the hands of priests but also from being dismissed, ignored, or even blamed by Church officials when they have presented their complaints. Second, the families of the victims have suffered from having their loved ones traumatized by a person and an institution that they thought that they could trust unconditionally. Third, there are many clerics who have been falsely accused and clerics who have done nothing wrong but, because they wear Roman collars, have been assumed to be sex offenders by the general public. And, of course, rank-and-file Catholics in the pews often feel demoralized and upset that their beloved Church has been scandalized for so many years with little hope for resolution. They often find it hard to continue donating their monies to Catholic parishes and charities, not wanting their hard-earned cash going to high-priced lawyers and others associated with the scandal. Catholics also find it hard to defend their Church and faith tradition from those who believe that the Church is hopelessly corrupt, flawed, and in the minds of many, evil.

These are the reasons that this book, *Healing Our Church*, is such a godsend. People of faith are desperately in need of a way to better understand and cope with the trauma that has unfolded in the Church for so long. They need a path toward peace, reconciliation, forgiveness, and wholeness. They need a way to hold onto their faith, even while knowing that many of the humans who represent the faith tradition have sinned and have stumbled in such egregious ways. This book is likely the best tool available to journey toward this much needed healing. It offers a pathway to healing, and it offers hope.

I, for one, have been working in this area for over 30 years. As an engaged daily-Mass kind of Catholic and as a clinical psychologist, I was approached by a priest friend in the 1980s who asked me to help with a few of his fellow priests who were accused of sexual misbehavior. I conducted a psychological evaluation and treatment plan and consulted with the religious order with which the priests were affiliated. Soon enough, more cases came my way from multiple religious orders and dioceses.

As a psychology professor at a Catholic university, I then sought out peers who were working in the area throughout the United States and Canada which led to collaborative research projects, consultation, and a book project. The book, *Bless Me Father for I Have Sinned: Perspectives on Sexual Abuse Committed by Roman Catholic Priests*, was published in 1999, several years before the famous *Boston Globe* story was published. Few people were interested in our work. In fact, we held a press conference during May 1998 at our university with compelling national and international data on the problem that we featured in our first book project, and only one member of the mainstream press (i.e., the *San Francisco Chronicle*) showed up—and that was because the reporter was a friend of our university media-relations director.

After the *Boston Globe* story was published in 2002, everything changed. Sexual abuse by Catholic clergy became a headline story, above the fold, in *The New York Times* each day for over 70 days. Media interest was everywhere. More research, consultations, requests for assessments and evaluations, books, and so forth unfolded at a rapid-fire pace. At this point,

I have evaluated and treated many victims of clergy abuse as well as many clerical offenders. I've served on the United States Conference of Catholic Bishops' National Review Board for child protection as well as on local diocesan and religious-order review boards for child protection. And I've talked with more local, national, and international media, in both the Catholic and secular press than I can possibly count. I'm immersed in this topic. This has become my world. Yet, I am hopeful and optimistic. I know that the clergy-abuse problem is a solvable one and, in my humble view, we are well underway toward our goal to ensure that children are safe in the Church and that those with a predilection toward sexually violating minors will stay out of ministry and never be ordained.

Why am I so optimistic? First, we have to look at what the Church has done since 2002. The incidents of clerical sexual abuse in recent decades are down to a trickle. Many of the newer abuse cases since 2002 have involved visiting international priests here on vacation, sabbatical, or studies; these priests have not undergone the training and screening that is required of American clerics. The U.S. Conference of Catholic Bishops' *Dallas Charter* and subsequent Church reforms have resulted in a number of industry-standard and even ground-breaking policies and procedures to keep children safe in Church-related activities as well as ways to keep abusing priests out of ministry. All dioceses and religious orders, as well as the bishops' conference have lay review boards with judges, lawyers, psychologists, social workers, human-resource professionals, law-enforcement officers, and so forth reviewing all reports of improper clerical behavior involving minors. And cases involving adult victims are now being reviewed. All church workers, including clerics, lay staff, and volunteers, must participate in safe-environment training that highlights signs and symptoms of abuse and details policies and procedures for keeping children safe and reporting clerical misbehavior. An independent auditing firm conducts yearly audits to ensure that all dioceses follow these guidelines and then makes its findings publicly known.

A zero-tolerance policy is now in effect that provides that any credible accusation of sexual abuse by clerics is reported to law enforcement, the offending cleric is withdrawn from ministry and evaluated by an expert in the area and, if accusations are found to be credible, the offending cleric never returns to ministry. Things are very different in the Church since 2002 than they were before 2002, and the outcome in terms of new cases is proof that these measures are indeed working. When you have well over 40,000 priests in the United States as well as many deacons and other church workers, some offenders may fall between the cracks. It is critically important to identify holes in the system and to carefully plug them. We are now doing so.

Keeping children and teens safe from sexual or any kind of abuse should be everyone's priority. Tragically, data suggests that whenever men, clerics or not, have access to and power over children and teens, a small percentage of them will violate that trust and sexually abuse these minors. The current version of the *Diagnostic and Statistical Manual* published by the American Psychiatric Association estimates that about five percent of men are pedophiles. This is true for Catholic and non-Catholic clerics as well as lay teachers, athletic coaches, tutors, choir directors, scout leaders, and so forth. This is tragically also true of fathers and step-fathers, brothers, and cousins. The best way to deal with this reality is to develop evidence-based best practices that create environments where children are safe and where people who wish to work with minors are carefully screened. Doing this has been very successful with many organizations during the past decade or so, including the Catholic Church, the Boy Scouts, Boys & Girls Clubs of America, and public and private schools. These organizations have consulted with each other (and I have participated in some of these meetings and conferences) to ensure that best practices are known and followed. Certainly, some offenders do fall between the cracks when policies and procedures are not followed carefully. And so, more work is always needed to be sure that these best practices and industry standards are followed at all times and by everyone.

The good news is that progress is being made to ensure that children are safe, but vigilance is critically needed, and good data and reason need to take precedence over emotion and hysteria if we truly want to keep children and families safe from abuse in the Church as well as in all institutions where adults and children interact. Sadly, the press rarely reports on these achievements in child safety and their reporting often leads one to believe that nothing has been done to solve the problem of clergy abuse in the Church. Good news and progress perhaps don't sell papers, but much progress has indeed been made and continues to occur. Of course, we need everyone in position of influence and authority in and out of the Church to help. This book will help us all to heal along the way and I, for one, am grateful for it.

Thomas G. Plante, Ph.D., ABPP
Santa Clara University and Stanford University School of Medicine

Facing the Truth

SESSION
ONE

INTRODUCTIONS

Leader: Invite participants to share what prompted them to join these sessions on Healing Our Church.

FOCUS

We acknowledge the sexual abuse by clergy, the enduring harm to victims, the coverup by Church leaders, and our feelings about these events.

PRAY

Song Suggestion: "God Will Wipe Away Every Tear," M.D. Ridge
© 1998, M.D. Ridge. Published by OCP. All rights reserved. Used with permission.
(To download, visit www.ocp.org/renew-music*)*

God will wipe away ev'ry tear,
God will wipe away ev'ry tear,
Ev'ry sorrow will end,
Ev'ry broken heart will be healed and
God will wipe away ev'ry tear.

Divide the group in two and pray:

Side 1: Compassionate God,
We come to you with feelings of anger, sadness, and betrayal.
We come to you with broken hearts as we grieve
for the victims of abuse
and for the coverups by Church leaders.

Side 2: Faithful God, while we may not be sure of many things,
we know that you are with us
in darkness and in light, today and every day,
always calling us to greater trust in you.

Side 1: Just God, may truth, justice, compassion and forgiveness
be the salve
that heals our wounded hearts and our broken Church.
Rebuild our trust and strengthen our faith.

Side 2: Spirit of the Living God, bless our time of prayer
and sharing of our faith, thoughts, and emotions.
Show us a path through this devastating time.
Empower us to play our role in healing and reforming
our Church.
© RENEW International

All: Come, Holy Spirit, fill the hearts of your faithful
and enkindle in them the fire of your love.
Send forth your Spirit, and they shall be created,
and you will renew the face of the earth.
O, God, who by the light of the Holy Spirit
did instruct the hearts of the faithful,
grant that by the same Holy Spirit we may be truly wise,
ever to rejoice in his consolations,
Through Christ Our Lord, Amen.

A Survivor's Story

"I was one of six boys in an Irish Catholic family. When I was ten years old, as a reward for doing well in my math test, my teacher sent me over to the rectory to assist a beloved parish priest in counting the Sunday collection. From that moment on, he sexually abused me consistently over two dozen times."

Reflection

This story from a small town near Pittsburgh, and thousands like it from around the country, have caused a seismic fault line in the faith of many practicing Catholics. Disillusioned by the current sexual-abuse scandal in the Catholic Church, one 87-year-old woman not only considered skipping Sunday Mass for the first time in more than six decades but considered leaving the Church altogether. Many have felt as she did; many have left the Church.

Although the problem of sexual abuse in the Church and coverup by bishops and others had been revealed many years before, an episode that especially rattled the faith and confidence of American Catholics was the 2018 report by a Pennsylvania state grand jury. The report listed more than 300 priests who had abused children over seven decades and who, for most of that time, had been protected by the hierarchy. The grand-jury report estimated that the victims numbered in the thousands.

The abuse of children and adults by priests, and the manner in which some of the clergy have responded is a truly horrific story—real, raw, and painful. The Church in Pennsylvania is not unique. We continue to hear of similar revelations and reactions from various parts of our country and in other countries, leaving us to wonder how pervasive the problem is.

A flood of emotions ensues among Catholics. When we hear this news, we may feel angry, betrayed, and shocked, or any of a host of other emotions.

We are horrified for those who have suffered as that boy from an Irish Catholic home suffered, and as the man he became has suffered ever since. We may explode in anger: "How dare anyone do such a thing to a child? How dare anyone do such a thing in our Church?" We may be bewildered as we try to understand these incidents—the exploitation of innocent victims and the attempts by the Church to conceal rather than confront the problem. We may even succumb to denial: "Surely, this is not true!" But we know that it is true, and that reality can lead some into depression.

Shock, alarm, denial, anger—these are all classic symptoms of loss and grief. And that is not surprising. After all, any experience of loss leads to grieving. And we might feel that we have indeed lost a loved one—lost not only our trust in the leadership of the Church but lost our Church itself.

How can we help ourselves and others deal with these feelings and find a way forward?

We must first acknowledge them and accept them—in ourselves and in others. As in any sense of loss and grieving, the feelings are central to our reconciliation and ultimately to action.

So, to begin our faith sharing on healing our Church, we ask the Spirit who prays within us to help us acknowledge and accept our feelings so that we may confront this scandal with a new understanding of who we are as Church and who God is calling us to become.

SHARE

*Take a few moments of silence to reflect on the following questions. Then share
your responses.*

1. What feelings or thoughts arise as you reflect on sexual abuse by clergy,
    the enduring harm to victims, and the coverup by Church leaders?

    *Apalling feelings for the heads of our church
    for the cover up of these disgusting acts*

2. How has the scandal affected your relationship with God—your
    prayer, your faith—and your feelings about the Church?

    *Relationship with God is strong I don't blame God
    These actions have caused me to step back
    and revisit my beliefs.*

THE WORD OF GOD

Reader: A reading from the Book of Lamentations (3:17-24)

My soul is bereft of peace;
    I have forgotten what happiness is;
so I say, "Gone is my glory,
    and all that I had hoped for from the Lord."

The thought of my affliction and my homelessness
    is wormwood and gall!
My soul continually thinks of it
    and is bowed down within me.
But this I call to mind,
    and therefore I have hope:

The steadfast love of the Lord never ceases,
    his mercies never come to an end;
they are new every morning;
    great is your faithfulness.
"The Lord is my portion," says my soul,
    "therefore I will hope in him."

The Word of the Lord.

All: Thanks be to God.

SHARE

Take a few moments of silence to reflect on the following question. Then share your responses:

In light of the theme of this session, what does the reading from the Book of Lamentations say to you?

_____

_____

_____

_____

REFLECTION

The Book of Lamentations in the Old Testament consists of five heart-wrenching poems written after the destruction of Jerusalem and its Temple by the Babylonians in the sixth century before the birth of Jesus Christ. Besides levelling the holy city, the Babylonians had carried a large segment of the population into exile, leaving behind only the poorest and weakest.

The poet cries out in suffering, grief, and anger—even directing these feelings toward God. Still, in the midst of her grief, Israel keeps a fundamental faith in God and his mercy. Ultimately, such faith gives these people the strength to endure their suffering and look forward to a better future.

As they gather over the ashes to grieve the tragedy that had befallen the community, the people stand together in prayer and ritual. Even as they weep and lament, they continue to ask for assistance, to praise God, and to recover their hope of rebuilding their shattered way of life. They know that it will not happen quickly or easily. Yet even in their darkest moments of grief, they continue to praise God with whom, they believe, all things are possible.

In our reaction to revelations of sexual abuse in the Church, we can recognize many of the feelings expressed in the victim's story that began this session and by the poet bewailing the calamity visited upon Israel. We lament the sins and crimes committed within our Church—the abuse itself and the attempts by Church leadership to hide it. We lament the harm done to children and adults whose lives have been permanently affected. We lament the broken trust, the loss of reverence we once had for priests and bishops, and the stigma borne by faithful priests and bishops in the Church.

But like the Israelites in Babylon, let us squarely face the reality— the sexual abuse and coverup—while continuing to have faith in God. Our God is faithful even when some ministers have proven unfaithful. Through our baptism, we are empowered to stand up against evil and remedy the unjust situation. Baptism imparts on us a prophetic role; in order for us to carry out this role, our faith in Jesus must be strong and unshakable. As we let our feelings play out in this difficult time, let us especially renew our faith in the Paschal Mystery—the suffering, death, and resurrection of Jesus—which reminds us that, although we who are the Church are suffering now, with the grace of God we can find a way forward.

Let us be confident that God will sustain us in our present grief and reform the Church through an empowered laity and a faithful clergy who together are the Body of Christ.

SHARE

Take a few moments of silence to reflect on one or more of the following points. Then share your responses:

1. What is your deepest lament over the clergy sexual abuse and cover up? Why is it important to face it squarely?

   The fact that it was covered up by trusted church officials

2. The people of Israel hoped for the restoration of Jerusalem and the Temple. What is your hope for the Church?

To become Stronger

ACT

In this session, we have faced the truth in order to move forward, faithful clergy and empowered laity, to transform the Church. How does this inspire you to act? Here are some examples:

1. If this session has raised serious issues or concerns for you, consider seeking professional guidance from a trusted advisor. Telephone hotlines that offer assistance are listed on page 88 of this book. Also, visit our website for resources that may help.

2. Pray for the victims of sexual abuse.

3. Ask your pastor to include in the Prayer of the Faithful at Sunday Mass a prayer for victims of any sexual abuse and a prayer for wisdom and courage for church leaders to address the scandal.

4. Visit your diocesan website and learn what policies are currently in place to protect children and adults from sexual abuse and to aid victims, and what your local bishop is personally doing to address this scandal.

5. If you have not done so, read the introduction to this book by psychologist Thomas Plante.

6. Read the *Charter for the Protection of Children and Young People*, a set of procedures first adopted in 2002, and revised since, by the United States Conference of Catholic Bishops to address allegations of sexual abuse by Catholic clergy and achieve reconciliation, healing, accountability, and prevention of future crimes. Find the link at pages. renewintl.org/healing-our-church-resources-page or visit www.usccb. org/issues-and-action/child-and-youth-protection/charter.cfm

PRAY

A PRAYER FOR THE HEALING OF OUR CHURCH

Pray together:

Good and gracious God,
We ask for healing for our wounded Church
and a way forward through this time of despair.

We cry out to you for healing for the victims of abuse
and for their families.
We cry out to you for healing for the lay faithful.
We cry out to you for healing for our clergy.

Grant our bishops the courage and wisdom
to work with the laity for the transformation of our Church.

Embrace your people with your compassionate mercy,
and restore our trust in the Church and its ministers.

Give us hope that the Church will be reformed by your grace
working in and through us.

May Jesus, the compassion and power of God,
draw us to himself in Word and Sacrament and send us forth
strengthened in faith to share his love with the world.

We ask this in the name of Jesus and through the power of the Holy Spirt,
one God for ever and ever. Amen.

© 2019 RENEW International

LOOKING AHEAD

Prepare for the next session by reading Mark 2:1-12.

Healing Our Wounds

SESSION TWO

FOCUS

Healing our wounds is possible, and we all have a role to play in that healing..

PRAY

Song Suggestion: "Loving and Forgiving," Scott Soper
©1992, OCP. All rights reserved. Used with permission.
(To download, visit **www.ocp.org/renew-music***)*

REFRAIN
Loving and forgiving are you, O Lord;
slow to anger, rich in kindness,
loving and forgiving are you.

Divide the group in two and pray:

Side 1:   God of endless love,
ever caring, ever strong,
always present, always just:
You gave your only Son
to save us by the blood of his cross.

Side 2:   Gentle Jesus, shepherd of peace,
join to your own suffering
the pain of all who have been hurt
in body, mind, and spirit
by those who betrayed the trust placed in them.

Side 1:   Hear our cries as we agonize
over the harm done to our brothers and sisters.
Breathe wisdom into our prayers,
soothe restless hearts with hope,
steady shaken spirits with faith:
Show us the way to justice and wholeness,
enlightened by truth and enfolded in your mercy.

Side 2:   Holy Spirit, comforter of hearts,
heal your people's wounds
and transform our brokenness.
Grant us courage and wisdom, humility and grace,
so that we may act with justice
and find peace in you.
We ask this through Christ, our Lord.

All: Amen.

A Survivor's Story

Thomas was 16 when he was first sexually assaulted by a priest at his local church in Nassau County, New York. Thomas, who had joined the church's youth ministry in search of guidance, told *The New York Times* that the abuse continued for 14 years until the priest died.

"I hate saying his name," said Thomas, who was 52 when he was interviewed. "I thought I had a father figure, you know, because my dad wasn't there. And he took advantage of me."

Much later, Thomas received a monetary settlement under a "compensation and reconciliation program" established by his diocese.

After revealing what the priest had done to him, Thomas left the Church for a few years, because he felt he had not received sufficient support. Despite his experience, however, and his continuing doubts about clergy in general and the hierarchy of the Church, he resumed attending Mass each week. He said that to allow the abuse inflicted on him to diminish his faith would be to let evil win.

Reflection

The Church, the Body of Christ, is wounded and in dire need of healing. And healing can happen when the whole Church—laity, religious, and clergy—talk openly together about what has happened, who has been harmed, and what must be done. Cardinal Blase J. Cupich of Chicago addressed this in September 2018 on the final evening of a novena for healing and justice for the victims of sexual abuse: "We can never again abandon victim-survivors. We must confront the truth, confront our own failures, and act to bring healing and justice to those who have been robbed of both."

We can do this, together, but we must recognize that healing is a process, not a one-time event. There are no quick fixes. Time and patience are essential to healing, and healing is different for each person. And always, the focus of healing must be the victims—those who have been directly harmed and those who have been betrayed, all of whom have wounds that endure. Often, the temptation in society is to run from the pain, to find quick solutions and move on. But our Christian faith tells us that for true healing to occur, we must embrace the pain, enter into it, move through it, and find ways to express it, trusting that we will come out on the other side full of hope. This is the promise of the death and resurrection of Jesus, to remember that "just as sin exercised dominion in death, so grace might also exercise dominion through justification leading to eternal life through Jesus Christ our Lord" (Romans 5:21).

Where sin abounds, it often leaves strong emotions in its wake. This became evident during a parish listening session: "I am in a rage over this situation," a young father cried, "I just keep thinking what if this were my child!" For healing to take place, all feelings must be not only accepted, but also honored. Anger, for example, can be a catalyst for change. As St. Augustine taught, "Hope has two beautiful daughters. Their names are Anger and Courage: anger at the way things are, and courage to see that they do not remain the way they are." As the parish listening session drew to a close, a woman reflected, "The hurt that's been done to people of faith by people of faith is really hard to come to terms with, but we need to heal together." "Yes," one of the parish sisters responded, "but true healing can only come with change." The Church needs to examine not only what happened, but also the flaws in the structure that allowed this sin to go on.

While Church leaders undertake that process, we are called to find and pursue our own roles as healers and reformers.

SHARE

Take a few moments of silence to reflect on the following questions. Then share your responses.

1. Describe a time when you experienced emotional or physical healing. What was that process like?

    _____

    _____

    _____

    _____

2. Reread the quote from St. Augustine. How might your anger and courage in the face of this scandal be a catalyst for healing?

    _____

    _____

    _____

    _____

THE WORD OF GOD

Reader: A reading from the Gospel According to Mark (2:1-12)

When he returned to Capernaum after some days, it was reported that he was at home. So many gathered around that there was no longer room for them, not even in front of the door; and he was speaking the word to them. Then some people came, bringing to him a paralyzed man, carried by four of them. And when they could not bring him to

Jesus because of the crowd, they removed the roof above him; and after having dug through it, they let down the mat on which the paralytic lay. When Jesus saw their faith, he said to the paralytic, "Son, your sins are forgiven." Now some of the scribes were sitting there, questioning in their hearts, "Why does this fellow speak in this way? It is blasphemy! Who can forgive sins but God alone?" At once Jesus perceived in his spirit that they were discussing these questions among themselves; and he said to them, "Why do you raise such questions in your hearts? Which is easier, to say to the paralytic, 'Your sins are forgiven,' or to say, 'Stand up and take your mat and walk'? But so that you may know that the Son of Man has authority on earth to forgive sins"—he said to the paralytic— "I say to you, stand up, take your mat and go to your home." And he stood up, and immediately took the mat and went out before all of them; so that they were all amazed and glorified God, saying, "We have never seen anything like this!"

The Gospel of the Lord.

All: Praise to you, Lord Jesus Christ.

SHARE

Take a few moments of silence to reflect on the following question. Then share your responses:

In light of the theme, "Healing Our Wounds," what does this passage say to you?

_____

_____

_____

_____

REFLECTION

The drama of Jesus healing a paralyzed man is magnified by the unique manner in which the man enters the house—lowered through the roof by four of his friends. Here we have a group of people who saw the need of the paralytic and were determined to help him. Rather than giving in to hopelessness and consigning him to his fate, they took extraordinary steps to bring him to the source of healing, Jesus. And, because of their determination, the man was made whole.

These people could not cure their friend on their own, but they knew they could contribute to his healing and, by doing so, they provide a model for us as we confront the scandal of sexual abuse and coverup. Like these people, we are not powerless in the face of the harm done to the victims of sexual abuse and to the Church. The scandal should not make us feel hopeless; ours is a faith of hope, of optimism, of falling and rising again, of death and resurrection.

With hope alive in us, we can bring the survivor victims to Jesus in prayer, asking on their behalf for interior peace and renewed trust in God; and we can bring the whole suffering Church to Jesus in prayer, asking for transparency and a renewed sense of compassion and justice. But, as the Letter of James reminds us (2:17), faith without works is dead. We who, together with the clergy, are the Body of Christ, are called to go beyond prayer and take action to help the victims and the Church emerge from this dark time.

If we are conditioned to think that we have no voice, or if we have been content to play a passive role, it helps to recall that Jesus' call to discipleship applies to all of us, and that many lay women and men have embraced that call and have contributed to renewal and reform in the Church.

A prominent example is Catherine of Siena, a saint of the 14th century, whose life was characterized by enormous charity and tireless energy for reform of the clergy and of the Church itself.

Catherine was a lay member of the Dominican order who, in a culture that did not empower women, saw the need for reform, judged what needed to be done, and acted to put pressure on Church leaders to be responsible. Like the friends of the paralytic man described in Mark's Gospel, Catherine would not accept the status quo, but instead took steps—even extraordinary steps—to help bring about healing.

Like other reformers, Catherine was dismayed by corruption in the Church. She believed that the problem stemmed in part from the fact that, because of the complicated politics among European states, the seat of the papacy had been moved from Rome to Avignon, France. So, the religious and administrative center of the Church was no longer in the holy city, and popes were under the influence of decadent aspects of French culture.

She was influential in convincing Pope Gregory XI to return the papacy to Rome; one of her many voluminous letters to him included an exhortation that resonates in our time: "Respond to the Holy Spirit who is calling you! I tell you: Come! Come! Come! Don't wait for time because time isn't waiting for you."

This is the most famous episode of Catherine's life, but it doesn't begin to describe the impact one person can have on the Church and on individual lives. She sent about four hundred letters to bishops, kings, scholars, merchants, and ordinary citizens. She interacted personally with many Church and secular leaders, but she also ministered directly to poor people and counselled those who were troubled in spirit. Just as God called

Catherine to this role, God calls us to be active participants in the life of the Church.

Addressing the crisis in the Church is not the business only of saints. Catherine herself urges us to "speak the truth in a million voices. It is silence that kills." We may not yet know how we can contribute to the healing of the Church, but Catherine's example tells us that we are called to have a role as members of the Body of Christ.

SHARE

Take a few moments of silence to reflect on one or more of the following points. Then share your responses.

1. As you consider the sexual-abuse scandal in the Church and reflect on the story of the healing of the paralyzed man, where do you picture yourself in the scene? With what character do you most identify? Why?

    _____

    _____

    _____

    _____

2. How does the example set by St. Catherine of Siena motivate you to act to help heal the Church?

    _____

    _____

    _____

    _____

ACT

In this session, we have acknowledged that healing the Church is possible and that we all can have a role in that healing. In what way does this inspire you to act? Here are some examples:

1. If this session has raised serious issues or concerns for you, consider seeking professional guidance from a trusted advisor. Telephone hotlines that offer assistance are listed on page 88 of this book. Also, visit our website for resources that may help.

2. Read the article "Safety and Prevention" on the RENEW International website: pages.renewintl.org/healing-our-church-resources-page.

3. Suggest to your pastor a healing and reconciliation service in your parish. Offer to help plan it. See our website, pages.renewintl.org/healing-our-church-resources-page for resources for planning.

4. Continue to pray for the victims of sexual abuse, for the healing of our Church, and for enlightenment and courage in order to act.

PRAY

A PRAYER FOR THE HEALING OF OUR CHURCH

Pray together:

Good and gracious God,
We ask for healing for our wounded Church
and a way forward through this time of despair.

We cry out to you for healing for the victims of abuse
and for their families.
We cry out to you for healing for the lay faithful.
We cry out to you for healing for our clergy.

Grant our bishops the courage and wisdom
to work with the laity for the transformation of our Church.

Embrace your people with your compassionate mercy,
and restore our trust in the Church and its ministers.

Give us hope that the Church will be reformed by your grace
working in and through us.

May Jesus, the compassion and power of God,
draw us to himself in Word and Sacrament and send us forth
strengthened in faith to share his love with the world.

We ask this in the name of Jesus and through the power of the Holy Spirt,
one God for ever and ever. Amen.

© 2019 RENEW International

LOOKING AHEAD

Prepare for the next session by reading St. Paul's Letter to the Ephesians 4:11-13, 15-16.

Rebuilding Our Church

SESSION
THREE

FOCUS

We identify and explore the factors leading to sexual abuse and coverup in the Church. We claim our role in rebuilding our Church.

PRAY

Song Suggestion: "O Jesus, Healer of Wounded Souls,"
Pedro Rubalcava. © 2001, Pedro Rubalcava. Published by OCP. All rights reserved.
Used with permission. *(To download, visit* <u>www.ocp.org/renew-music</u>*)*

REFRAIN
O Jesus, healer of wounded souls,
come heal us.
Touch us and make us whole; heal our world.
Raise your people to life.

Pray together:

Lord, make me an instrument of your peace:
where there is hatred, let me sow love;
where there is injury, pardon;
where there is doubt, faith;

where there is despair, hope;
where there is darkness, light;
where there is sadness, joy.

O divine Master, grant that I may not so much seek
to be consoled as to console,
to be understood as to understand,
to be loved as to love.
For it is in giving that we receive,
it is in pardoning that we are pardoned,
and it is in dying that we are born to eternal life.
Amen.

A Survivor's Story

Donna Harper's son was a victim of sexual abuse by a priest, but Donna still has faith in the Church and is doing her part to address such crimes. Donna's son, who has left the Church, told her of the abuse in 1999 when the priest involved was arrested for other offenses. The priest, who had been assigned to the Harpers' parish, was sentenced to prison after pleading guilty to raping a teenage boy after leaving the priesthood. But the prosecutor told *The Tennessean*, a daily newspaper in Nashville, that the priest had abused about 30 boys over more than two decades, and that the diocese was aware of such behavior but did not report it to police. Donna Harper's son had been one of those victims.

In an interview with *The Tennessean*[*], Donna said she was angry with her diocese for having protected the priest. Even so, when the bishop of Nashville asked her to serve on the diocesan review board, she accepted and has served for more than 15 years. Diocesan boards were created

---

[*] *The Tennessean*, September 1, 2018

after the United States Conference of Catholic Bishops (USCCB) adopted the *Charter for the Protection of Children and Young People* in June 2002. The diocesan boards are made up mostly of lay people who are not employees of the diocese. Each board also includes an experienced pastor, an expert on the treatment of child sex abuse, and often a victim or family member of a victim. The role of this board is to advise the bishop in his evaluation of charges and evidence of sexual abuse of minors by clergy; advise him in determining whether a priest who has been accused is fit for ministry; and review diocesan policies on these issues.

Besides creating national and diocesan review boards, the *Charter*, which has been revised several times, imposed several obligations on dioceses, including these:

- to report to law-enforcement authorities any credible accusation of sexual abuse of a minor;
- to cooperate in the investigation;
- to heal and promote reconciliation of abuse survivors and their families;
- to investigate a charge of sexual abuse even if a statute of limitations prevents criminal prosecution;
- to remove a priest from ministry—possibly even from the priesthood— if even a single case of child abuse is admitted or proven;
- to create a safe environment for children through screening and training of ministers and other personnel.

Donna Harper said she converted to Catholicism in 1964 while she was in junior high school. She thinks she has stayed in the Church because she chose it rather than being born into it. "I stay with the basic teachings," she said, "and pray for healing."

REFLECTION

No single factor leads to the kind of crime and coverup that ensnared Donna and her son and thousands of other victims and their families. As Bishop Robert Barron, founder of *Word on Fire*, has said, "Anything as complex as this phenomenon has multiple causes. … Almost every event has multiple causes."

Some misconceptions have arisen about the factors leading to sexual abuse of children by priests, including the roles of celibacy and homosexuality. Research by the John Jay College of Criminal Justice, commissioned by the USCCB, stresses the complexity of the issue and offers multiple factors leading to these crimes. The researchers conclude that there is no direct connection between celibacy or homosexuality and the abuse of children in the Church; being celibate or homosexual did not increase the risk that a priest would violate children.

Thomas G. Plante, professor of psychology at Santa Clara University, wrote in *America* magazine in October 2018 that sexual orientation, by itself, is not a risk factor for sexual crimes against minors or, for that matter, against anyone. Dr. Plante cited the John Jay College team's conclusion that "most of the clergy sexual offenders were … men who simply abused victims to whom they had access and with whom they had the opportunity to develop trust. In the Catholic Church, these individuals tended to be boys. … Boys were trusted with priests."

The John Jay study, in fact, reported that most of the clergymen who committed these offenses in the latter 20th century would describe themselves as more likely heterosexual.

The report explained that the incidents of sexual abuse per year "increased steadily from the mid-1960s through the late 1970s, then declined in the 1980s and continue to remain low." It added that the majority of priests accused of abuse from 1950 to 2002 were ordained between the 1950s and the 1970s.

The researchers found that "many accused priests began abusing years after they were ordained, at times of increased job stress, social isolation, and decreased contact with peers." In addition, there were only a few resources in place—such as professional counseling, with its limits—to help them with their difficulties. "Priests who lacked close social bonds . . . were more likely to sexually abuse minors than those who had a history of close social bonds," the report said.

The John Jay researchers wrote that while the response to the sexual-abuse crisis concentrated for a long time on the characteristics of the offenders, it did not adequately address factors in the structure of the Church that enabled abuse and protected abusers. From their perspective, as from Bishop Barron's, clericalism and the abuse of power have played an important role in these crimes.

"Clericalism" refers to a culture in which some clergy assume an attitude of superiority and privilege to which they are not entitled. It is an attitude that the laity have, for generations, been unable or unwilling to challenge. Pope Francis has referred to this attitude repeatedly, and he, too, has made the connection between a clergy that lords it over the laity and the crimes of sexual abuse. In August 2018, the pope told a group of Jesuits in Dublin, "This drama of abuse, especially when it is widespread and gives great scandal … has behind it a Church that is elitist and clericalist, an inability to be near to the people of God."

In that same month, in a letter "to the people of God," Pope Francis stressed that the Church consists of all its members—laity and clergy—and he warned that the Church cannot move forward if that is not clearly understood and implemented in practice. Francis wrote, "This is clearly seen in a peculiar way of understanding the Church's authority, one common in many communities where sexual abuse and the abuse of power and conscience have occurred. … Clericalism, whether fostered by priests themselves or by lay persons … supports and helps to perpetuate many of the evils that we are condemning today. To say 'no' to abuse is to say an emphatic 'no' to all forms of clericalism."

The John Jay report referred to abuse of power within other organizations—for example, within police departments. The study said that factors, such as those contributing to police brutality, have also existed in the Church and help to explain "how the abuse of minors was able to persist within the organization for so many years."

"The police subculture is such," the report said, "that officers are reluctant to report fellow officers for deviant or criminal behavior, largely out of fear of ostracism by their peers. While some officers do report their colleagues, many instances of police misconduct and deviance are revealed via a publicized scandal. . . . Often police administrators are reluctant to acknowledge the existence of criminal or deviant behavior prior to its public exposure. This pattern is not unique to the police or other organizations and is quite similar to the behavior of priests in the Catholic Church."

The John Jay College report notes that since 2002 "the Catholic Church has taken serious steps toward understanding and reducing the problem of sexual abuse of minors by priests." The report mentions the *Dallas Charter* which includes guidelines for reconciliation, healing, accountability, and prevention of future acts of abuse. The report says that the U.S. bishops are "continuing through the model of organizational change and are on their way to implementing what are considered to be best practices in terms of education about abuse."

At their June 2018 Plenary Assembly, the bishops identified and discussed in depth issues that were not adequately addressed in the *Dallas Charter*. For example,

- The "zero tolerance" principle in the charter has applied to priests (one offense results in removal from ministry) but not to bishops who have committed abuse. Also, there is no clear policy addressing bishops who have not acted responsibly to reports of clergy abuse.

- There is a need for greater transparency in how allegations of abuse are dealt with by dioceses.

- There is a need for better auditing and accountability; some bishops have not been as vigilant as others in making sure all aspects of the charter are being applied.

- The term "vulnerable adults" should apply not only to those with special needs, as canon law describes them; but also to those over whom bishops or priests have power—for example, bishops over seminarians or priests over parishioners.

Individual dioceses have also taken steps to become more responsive to victims, more responsible about reporting suspected abusers, and more transparent about these activities. New Jersey dioceses, for instance, formed a compensation program for child victims of clerical abuse. This program will assist dioceses with financial resources to provide compensation and counseling for those who were victims as minors. As Cardinal Joseph Tobin, archbishop of Newark, explained to the World Meeting of Families in Dublin, August 2018, "This will give victims a formal voice and allow them to be heard by an independent panel. … The program also will assure that victims who have not received any financial compensation will be paid, regardless of whether their claims meet the time requirements of the statute of limitations."

SHARE

Take a few moments of silence to reflect on the following. Then share your responses.

1. Why do you think it is important for someone like Donna, who has been directly affected by clergy abuse, to be a member of the diocesan review board?

_____

_____

_____

_____

2. Discuss the factors contributing to the coverup of sexual abuse in the Church or elsewhere.

_____

_____

_____

_____

3. Which of the loopholes in the Charter do you think the bishops need to immediately address?

Immediate action _____

_____

_____

_____

The Word of God

Reader: A reading from St. Paul's Letter to the Ephesians (4:11-13, 15-16)

The gifts he gave were that some would be apostles, some prophets, some evangelists, some pastors and teachers, to equip the saints for the work of ministry, for building up the body of Christ, until all of us come to the unity of the faith and of the knowledge of the Son of God, to maturity, to the measure of the full stature of Christ. … (S)peaking the truth in love, we must grow up in every way into him who is the head, into Christ, from whom the whole body, joined and knit together by every ligament with which it is equipped, as each part is working properly, promotes the body's growth in building itself up in love.

The Word of the Lord.

All: Thanks be to God.

Share

Take a few moments of silence to reflect on the following question. Then share your response:

In light of the theme of this session, what does the reading from Paul's Letter to the Ephesians say to you?

_____

_____

_____

_____

REFLECTION

Powerful words from St. Paul describe how each of us is a part of the Body of Christ—our Church. And each of us is called not only to be a part of the Body but also to be an active member, each contributing his or her own perspective and gifts to build up and, when necessary, to heal our Church.

This is a concept that St. Francis of Assisi came to understand, and it became the basis for his life's work.

Francis, whose father was a wealthy spice and cloth merchant, turned away from a carefree life in favor of a life of simplicity and service to the poor—a life he believed to be the only way to follow Christ. Francis was praying in a neglected wayside chapel dedicated to St. Damiano when, he reported, he had a vision of Christ telling him, "Francis, Francis, go and repair my house which, as you can see, is falling into ruins." Francis took this call literally and immediately sold a load of his father's drapery and even his horse to raise money to rebuild that chapel—eventually doing the physical labor himself, and he attended to the repair of other chapels.

But Francis saw a broader meaning to "repair my house." Dismissed by some as a fool or lunatic, Francis, through his self-imposed poverty, set an example for the whole Church which, at the time, was ostentatiously wealthy and preoccupied with the sometimes-violent suppression of heresies. Francis gathered followers, a movement of the laity that involved recommitting to the Gospel by living simply with a focus on Christ and the poor. He founded the order now known as the Friars Minor while he was still a layman. He was later ordained a deacon.

Francis of Assisi continues to inspire and challenge Christians and non-Christians today. If we follow his example, we will not be content to respond with silence or resignation to the damage that has been done to the Church, the people of God—victims and their families, the lay faithful, and faithful clergy. Rather, we will respond to the call to build up God's reign on earth; we will discern our role in repairing the damage, and we will act. Some actions may come quickly to mind; some may come only after prayer or after dialogue and collaboration with others. However we discern it, we have a role in healing our Church. These are some examples:

- explore with the pastor ways the parish can make clear its compassion for those affected by sexual abuse;

- pray for victims of sexual abuse privately and as a parish;

- encourage the pastor to hold "listening sessions" and provide other means of enabling people to express their emotions and seek healing;

- press church leaders to include lay women and men in the process of acknowledging complaints.

Participate in the *Protecting God's Children* course offered by your diocese[1], so you are better trained to identify sexual abuse in the Church, in a family, or in any organization that serves children and teenagers.

As Paul wrote to the Christians in Ephesus, and as he writes elsewhere, every "ligament" in the Body of Christ has a role, and, like Francis and Catherine of Siena, like Donna Harper of Nashville, we are all called to discern our role and fulfill it. May we be empowered by remembering that Jesus called together an assembly of people focused on him—his teaching and his example—not a top-to-bottom structure in which some have more of a stake than others. We are the Church.

---

[1] For information about this program, visit your diocese's website or **www.virtusonline.org**.

SHARE

Take a few moments of silence to reflect on one or more of the following points. Then share your responses.

1. Paul wrote about the "ligaments" in the Body of Christ. How do you see yourself fitting that description?

    _____

    _____

    _____

    _____

2. What can we do to heal the wounds and rebuild the Church? What changes need to be made?

    _____

    _____

    _____

    _____

3. Name the actions that you think are most critical for the bishops to address. What questions would you like to ask your bishop?

    _____

    _____

    _____

    _____

ACT

In this session, we have reflected on factors leading to sexual abuse and coverup and our role in rebuilding the Church. How does this inspire you to act? Here are some examples:

1. As a group, write down the actions you think are most critical for your bishop to address regarding sexual abuse in the Church, what questions you would like him to answer, or what issues you would like him to clarify. Give your responses to your *Healing Our Church* coordinator so they can be combined with responses from the other small groups in your parish and sent to the bishop.

2. Register for the *Protecting God's Children* course offered by your diocese.

3. Continue to pray for victims of sexual abuse and for enlightenment about what actions you can take to help heal our Church.

4. If you are a mental-health professional or have a particular skill in the areas of abuse, consider volunteering to assist at the parish or diocesan level.

5. Go to pages.renewintl.org/healing-our-church-resources-page and read one of the articles related to this session of *Healing Our Church*.

PRAY

A Prayer for the Healing of Our Church

Pray together:
Good and gracious God,
We ask for healing for our wounded Church
and a way forward through this time of despair.

We cry out to you for healing for the victims of abuse
and for their families.
We cry out to you for healing for the lay faithful.
We cry out to you for healing for our clergy.

Grant our bishops the courage and wisdom
to work with the laity for the transformation of our Church.

Embrace your people with your compassionate mercy,
and restore our trust in the Church and its ministers.

Give us hope that the Church will be reformed by your grace
working in and through us.

May Jesus, the compassion and power of God,
draw us to himself in Word and Sacrament and send us forth
strengthened in faith to share his love with the world.

We ask this in the name of Jesus and through the power of the Holy Spirt,
one God for ever and ever. Amen.

LOOKING AHEAD

Prepare for the next session by reading the Gospel according to John 6:53, 60, 66-68.

Why Do I Remain a Catholic?

SESSION FOUR

Focus

We consider why Catholics have chosen to remain in the Church and articulate our own reasons for remaining Catholic.

Pray

Song Suggestion: "Do Not Fear to Hope," Rory Cooney.
©1985, OCP. All rights reserved. Used with permission.
(To download, visit <u>www.ocp.org/renew-music</u>*)*

REFRAIN
Do not fear to hope, though the wicked rage and rise.
Our God sees not as we see; success is not the prize.
Do not fear to hope, for though the night be long,
the race shall not be to the swift, the fight not to the strong.

Divide the group in two and pray:
Side 1:   God of hope and healing,
we know you are with us.
Make us more aware of your guidance
as we wrestle with
the sins of church ministers,

the pain that has been inflicted on the innocent,
and our disillusionment and despair.

All: "Lord, to whom can we go? You have the words of eternal life."

Side 2: God of hope and healing,
have mercy on the whole Church
and let this time of scandal become an opportunity
for real change in both our individual hearts
and in the Church as institution, through our efforts
and empowered by your Holy Spirit.

All: "Lord, to whom can we go? You have the words of eternal life."

Side 1: God of hope and healing,
thank you for the gift of the Eucharist
and the other sacraments
that open the door to the sacred,
touching us at the most important moments of our lives.
Thank you for the gift of the Scriptures,
your word that comes to us through the Prophets and Psalms,
your word in which we encounter Jesus.
Thank you for the faith we experience
in the community of believers.

All: "Lord, to whom can we go? You have the words of eternal life."

Side 2: God of hope and healing,
help us to hold fast to the richness
of our Catholic faith
and not lose sight of the many faithful laity,
religious, and clergy who continue your mission
of preaching the gospel, caring for the sick,
the needy, and all of creation, and fighting for social justice.

All: **"Lord, to whom can we go? You have the words
of eternal life."**

Side 1: God of hope and healing,
bring us into a deeper solidarity and communion
as the Body of Christ, as we remain faithful
to our relationship with you, seeking holiness
and recommitting ourselves to Jesus' mission
through charitable works and acts of justice,
taking part in the transformation of the Church and world.

All: **"Lord, to whom can we go? You have the words
of eternal life." Amen.**
© RENEW International

SHARE

Briefly share the reasons you have chosen to remain Catholic despite the sexual-abuse scandal.

_____

_____

_____

_____

A Survivor's Story

Michael Hoffman was born and raised a Catholic. As he was growing up, he and his family were very active in their parish in Lake Forest, Illinois. Michael was an altar server; that provided the opportunity for the priest in charge of the program to sexually abuse him and other boys while Michael was between the ages of 12 and 16.

And yet, Michael told the *Chicago Tribune*[2], he considers the Catholic community the "fabric" of his life. In fact, he leads a group that plans an annual "hope and healing Mass" in the Archdiocese of Chicago to acknowledge both the harm inflicted by abusers and the healing that has taken place.

Michael, now in his 50s, experienced "family dysfunction, anxiety, mild depression, and a broken heart" as a result of the abuse.[3] He did not discuss what had happened to him until 2006. He then told his wife, who is also a Catholic, and he told his pastor at their Chicago parish. Michael told the *Tribune* he was aware that the conversation with his pastor could have gone sour if the priest thought his own ministry or character were under attack. But instead, the pastor handled the matter in "a very good and gracious way."

Michael, a victim and survivor, never left the Church. He and his wife wanted to raise their two children—both of whom were altar servers—in the faith. Regarding the children, who are now adults, Michael told the *Tribune*, "What I've tried to do is tell them, even if abuse occurred

---

[2] "Former altar boy sexually abused by priest, tells why he's raising his kids in the Catholic Church," by Lauren Chval, *Chicago Tribune*, October 26, 2018.

[3] *The Healing Voices: Faith, Recovery, Reconciliation*, published for the United States Conference of Catholic Bishops' General Assembly, Baltimore, Maryland, November 2018.

in the Catholic Church and I'm one of the victims, good and healthy God-blessed things can actually happen here too."

One of those things is the annual healing Mass, which results from the combined efforts of abuse survivors, their loved ones, and clergy. Many of the participants, Michael told the *Tribune*, are "overcoming very painful memories, trauma, depression, anxiety …. They walk through that door, and they're participating in something in common. It fits with my Catholic faith."

Michael is a co-founder and co-editor of *The Healing Voices Magazine*[4], published by abuse survivors, which aims to create a dialogue among all who have been affected by child abuse in the Church. The publication contains testimonies and resources designed to help people seeking healing and reconciliation.

An issue published specifically for U.S. Catholic bishops said that "survivors and family members are returning from the desert, able to be wounded healers in their own circles."

REFLECTION

The term "wounded healer" is derived from the title of a work by the theologian Fr. Henri Nouwen[5] who wrote: "We all are wounded people, whether physically, emotionally, mentally, or spiritually. The main question is not, 'How can we hide our wounds?' so we don't have to be embarrassed, but, 'How can we put our woundedness into the service of others?' When our wounds cease to be a source of shame, and become a source of healing, we have become wounded healers."

---

[4] https://thehealingvoices.wordpress.com/

[5] *The Wounded Healer: Ministry in Contemporary Society*, © 1972 Henri J.M. Nouwen, Doubleday, New York, N.Y.

The experience of Michael Hoffman and hundreds of others dramatizes a reality that has been evident since Jesus' lifetime. The followers of Jesus are human—they blunder, they fail, they even commit crimes—but the faithful disciples must go on preaching and living the Gospel.

Even before the Church was instituted, this reality surfaced, for example, in the ambition of James and John, the duplicity of Judas, and the weakness and dishonesty of Peter.

James and John asked Jesus to promise them places of honor in his reign. Judas stole from the apostles' common funds and then betrayed Jesus in exchange for silver. And Peter, as Jesus had predicted, denied three times that he even knew the Lord.

But James, John, and Peter overcame their weaknesses and helped spread the faith through the known world.

In the history of the Church, there have been many serious forms of abuse. Forced conversions, for example, began as early as the fourth century under the Roman Emperor Constantine and have occurred in many parts of the world, including the Americas. Formal processes to combat heresy in Europe and campaigns to secure Christian holy sites in the Middle East, while they were well intended, sometimes resulted in extreme and unjust measures. And there are multiple examples of popes and other high-ranking churchmen who engaged in warfare, practiced nepotism, and violated their vows, living extravagantly and bearing children out of wedlock.

But despite crimes and excesses, the Church has consisted largely of committed lay women and men, dedicated religious, and faithful clergy whose goal has been to worship God, love one another, and seek out and care for those in need. Abuses and excesses have never changed the essence of our Church. It has remained the community Jesus gathered around himself, a community infused with the Holy Spirit, a community in which each of us is an equal member, and a community Jesus commissioned to be a source of hope and mercy for the whole world.

SHARE

Take a few moments of silence to reflect on the following. Then share your responses:

1. How is Michael Hoffman a wounded healer?

_____

_____

_____

_____

2. Why is it important to acknowledge the sins and crimes of the Church throughout history?

_____

_____

_____

_____

3. Share about a lay minister, religious or clergy person who gives you hope for the Church and inspires you to live your faith. Explain.

_____

_____

_____

_____

THE WORD OF GOD

Reader: A reading from the holy Gospel according to John
(6:53, 60, 66-68)

So Jesus said to them, "Very truly, I tell you, unless you eat the flesh of the Son of Man and drink his blood, you have no life in you. . . ." When many of his disciples heard it, they said, "This teaching is difficult; who can accept it?" … Because of this many of his disciples turned back and no longer went about with him. So Jesus asked the twelve, "Do you also wish to go away?" Simon Peter answered him, "Lord, to whom can we go? You have the words of eternal life."

The Gospel of the Lord.

All: Praise to you, Lord Jesus Christ.

SHARE

Take a few moments of silence to reflect on the following question. Then share your responses:

1. In light of this session's theme, what does the above passage from John say to you?

_____

_____

_____

_____

2. What are the "words of eternal life" that help you stay grounded in faith?

_____

_____

_____

_____

REFLECTION

Some disciples abandoned Jesus because they could not accept the idea of consuming his body and blood. People since then have left the Church, for other reasons—some trivial, some serious—and now some people have left or consider leaving because of the sexual crimes and the scandalous attempts to hide them. This decision is understandable, on the part of those who have been directly affected by the abuse and also on the part of those whose faith in the Church has been shaken by the scandal.

But many, perhaps asking Peter's question— "To whom can we go?"—have remained in the Church despite their feelings of anger, disappointment, or betrayal. We see many of those people at Mass. Although simple inertia may explain why some Catholics don't abandon the Church, others have made a conscious choice, naming specific characteristics of the Church as the answers to Peter's question. These are some of those characteristics:

- belief in the Incarnation and Resurrection of Jesus Christ, who dwells with us and in whom we find eternal life;

- baptism, the Eucharist, and the other sacraments;

- the continuity of the Church's mission, beginning with the first disciples;

- the truth of the Church's teachings;

- the Church as an assembly of people who share both faith and mission;

- the Church as a medium of forgiveness, hope, and renewal;

- the Church as the world's most potent voice for social justice and largest source of aid to people in need.

Mary Ann Steutermann, director of campus ministry at a Catholic high school in Louisville, Kentucky, is an example of someone who consciously chose to remain in the Church. She wrote that she made that decision because "the core tenets of the faith— the Incarnation and the Resurrection—shape my understanding of the world. God is truly present in human life, not only … in the person of Jesus but also in every conceivable life-giving and love-affirming moment of our own lives. And because of this sacredness of the human experience, life will always win in the end. … New life is always possible."[6]

Mary Ann's decision is not a passive or naïve acceptance of the failures of the Church as a religious institution. In fact, she wrote, one reason she stays is because she believes that "the only way to effect change to a system is from within it." And while she will pray for everyone affected by the abuse, she intends to press for change. She will speak out—for reform in civil law and Church practices, concrete actions by the leadership of the Church, a comprehensive study of abuse of power in the Church and genuine openness to "new possibilities for executing its pastoral mission." And she will call for transparency in all of these things.

---

[6] "Why I'm Staying Catholic in the Face of the Clergy Abuse Scandal," *Busted Halo* (https://bustedhalo.com), September 24, 2018.

Jacques David, who attends a parish in Brooklyn Heights, New York, is another Catholic who has remained in the Church despite his disappointment in the way the leadership has responded to sexual abuse. He told *The New York Times* that he thinks Catholics are accustomed to being told by authorities "how it's going to be."[7]

"Christ lives and dwells in us," Jacques said. "And so I think, as lay people, we have a sense of what is right and what is wrong. I think it's time for us to stand up and say, 'This is unacceptable.'"

He said he and his wife are raising their two children in both the Catholic and evangelical traditions, and he particularly wants the children to learn to apply Catholic social teaching through service and charity. So, as dismayed as he is by crimes and coverups, he won't allow the failures of others to drive him from his spiritual home.

"The one thing I remember my dad telling me, as a young boy," Jacques told *The Times*, "is: 'Don't let others cause you to lose your salvation.' I never understood what he meant by that. But as I've grown older, and now that I have children, I understand a little more."

Although the scandal that has disaffected many Catholics has been caused by priests and bishops, Professor Tiziana Dearing pointed out during a panel discussion at Boston College that the ministry of faithful priests has helped her maintain her faith and identity as a Catholic Christian.[8]

---

[7] "Why They Stay. Why They Can't: New York Catholics Wrestle with Their Faith Over Abuse Allegations," by Luis Ferré-Sadurní and Mariana Alfaro, *The New York Times*, October 23, 2018.

[8] ""Why I Remain A Catholic: Reflections on belief in a time of turmoil draw hundreds to Boston College's Robsham Theater," by Ed Hayward, University Communications, BC News (https://www.bc.edu/bc-web/bcnews/faith-religion/jesuit-catholic/c21-forum-belief-in-a-time-of-turmoil.html), January 4, 2019.

Noting that parish priests have been the focal point of the scandal, Professor Dearing added that part of the reason her faith is so deep is the influence of two priests, Fr. William Fitzgerald and Fr. J. Bryan Hehir. "Their roles in my life and formation have had profound sticking power for my faith," she said, "and I want to honor them and acknowledge them."

She also said that her Catholicism is the source of her knowledge of God: "I don't ever want to be disconnected from God. My Catholicism: the sacraments, the practice of faith in community, and Mass are [all examples of] how I know God."

And, she said, every aspect of her life is "animated by the social mission that Christ handed down to us"—a social mission that is at the heart of contemporary Catholic teaching.

There are many stories like these, and a theme that arises in many of them is a distinction between the Church as a human institution that will always have to strive for perfection and the Church as the Body of Christ made visible in the assembly in which we worship and with which we carry on the mission entrusted to us by Jesus. We can work to repair the institution, but if we leave the Body of Christ, "to whom can we go?"

SHARE

Take a few moments of silence to reflect on one or more of the following points. Then share your responses.

1. Which one of the statements by the people in the section above most resonate with your experience? How?

_____

_____

_____

_____

2. What are some reasons why Catholics decide to leave the Church? What would you say to someone who has made that choice?

_____

_____

_____

_____

3. Why do you remain Catholic despite the sexual-abuse scandal? Has this session helped you to articulate your answer? If so, how?

_____

_____

_____

_____

ACT

In this session, we have reflected on why Catholics have chosen to remain in the Church and we have articulated our own reasons for remaining Catholic. How does this inspire you to act? Here are some examples:

1. Write down why you remain Catholic. Share it with someone in the coming week.

2. Ask someone who is not in your small group why he or she remains Catholic.

3. Jot down all the reasons people in your group remain Catholic, add these to the responses from the other small groups in your parish and ask the pastor to put them in the bulletin.

4. Read the following article from *America: The Jesuit Journal* by a young mother, Kerry Weber, who is an executive editor for *America*: "What can I say to my kids when they ask why we keep faith in this Church?" August 15, 2018. Find the article at <ins>pages.renewintl.org/healing-our-church-resources-page</ins>.

5. Go to <ins>pages.renewintl.org/healing-our-church-resources-page</ins> and read one of the other articles related to this session of *Healing Our Church*.

PRAY

A PRAYER FOR THE HEALING OF OUR CHURCH

Pray together:
Good and gracious God,
We ask for healing for our wounded Church
and a way forward through this time of despair.

We cry out to you for healing for the victims of abuse
and for their families.
We cry out to you for healing for the lay faithful.
We cry out to you for healing for our clergy.

Grant our bishops the courage and wisdom
to work with the laity for the transformation of our Church.

Embrace your people with your compassionate mercy,
and restore our trust in the Church and its ministers.

Give us hope that the Church will be reformed by your grace
working in and through us.

May Jesus, the compassion and power of God,
draw us to himself in Word and Sacrament and send us forth
strengthened in faith to share his love with the world.

We ask this in the name of Jesus and through the power of the Holy Spirt,
one God for ever and ever. Amen.
© 2019 RENEW International

LOOKING AHEAD

Prepare for the next session by reading Colossians 3:12-17.

We Believe

SESSION
FIVE

FOCUS

Because of our faith in Christ, we are called to live as Christ.

PRAY

Song Suggestion: "Sing a New Church into Being," Dolores Dufner, OSB.
Text © 1991, The Sisters of St. Benedict. Published by OCP. All rights reserved. Used with permission. Music: NETTLETON; J. Wyeth's Repository of Sacred Music, Pt. 11, 1813.
(To download, visit www.ocp.org/renew-music*)*

REFRAIN
Let us bring the gifts that differ.
And, in splendid, varied ways,
Sing a new church into being,
One in faith and love and praise.

Ask members of the group, in turn, to read the petitions:

Leader: Almighty and most loving God, through your Son you brought compassion, healing and hope to our world. In this time of pain and confusion, we ask you to receive these petitions from your people. In these words, we renew our faith in your power to heal victims, to heal the wounds of your Church, and to draw all of us into a new era of safety and trust. We need you. We trust you. We place our needs before you:

Reader: For those who have been abused: That they may experience healing from shame, isolation, anger, and despair; that they may be listened to with compassion, treated with dignity, and supported in the healing process. We pray,

All: **Have mercy on us, Lord.**

Reader: For those who counsel victims: That their words of wisdom and compassion may be instruments of healing for those they accompany. We pray,

All: **Have mercy on us, Lord.**

Reader: For the perpetrators of abuse: That they may experience sincere remorse for their crimes, approach God with sorrow, and be prepared to make reparation for the damage they have caused. We pray,

All: **Have mercy on us, Lord.**

Reader: For those who failed to protect children, those who, in any way, betrayed the trust placed in them: May they humbly acknowledge their responsibility for harm done to children. We pray,

All: **Have mercy on us, Lord.**

Reader: For the faithful who are angry, scandalized, discouraged: That they may come to recognize the real presence of Christ in His Church despite the tragic failures of Church members and leaders. We pray,

All: **Have mercy on us, Lord.**

Reader: For all the faithful: That our response to this dark episode will result in even stronger faith that Christ will rebuild His Church and not allow evil to prevail; may we grow in our conviction that where sin abounds, grace abounds all the more; and may we renew our commitment to participate in the sacraments, learn the faith, join our parish communities, and serve the poor and marginalized. We pray,

All: **Have mercy on us, Lord.**

Reader: For our priests: That they may be protected from discouragement and that they may experience a renewal of authentic priestly identity, intimate union with Christ, joyful zeal for souls, liberating chastity, and humble charity. We pray,

All: **Have mercy on us, Lord.**

Reader: For our bishops: That they may take initiatives which: protect the flock entrusted to their care, restore trust, are transparent and free of self-interest, and unite the flock with the Heart of the Shepherd. We pray,

All: **Have mercy on us, Lord.**[9]

Leader: Loving God, we come to you to ask for mercy, for you are Mercy itself. We make our prayer in the name of your Son, our Lord Jesus Christ, who lives and reigns with you, in the unity of the Holy Spirit, one God, forever and ever. Amen.

---

[9] Prayer by Rev. Nicholas Rouch. Reprinted with permission from the Diocese of Erie, 2018.

A Survivor's Story

We begin this session with the story of one person who over a long period was able to move to forgiveness. Forgiveness is a decision but also a process that takes time, talk, and prayer. It will take some people much longer than others to arrive at this decision; that's to be expected. Forgiveness is a choice made daily with various degrees of strength, given the intensity of the struggle to deal with the consequences of abuse. Listen to this story and to whatever it stirs in your heart:

Pat has been a strong Catholic all her life, even though she was abused by a priest for three months when she was five years of age. She told the *Denver Catholic* newspaper[10] that her memory of the abuse was repressed for many years: "I had no [recollection] of it at all until I was 48 years old," Pat said. Meanwhile, she dealt with clinical depression throughout her life, and the condition worsened in 2001.

The following year, she sat in church listening to her pastor read a letter from the archbishop of Denver regarding the sexual-abuse scandal that had broken in the Archdiocese of Boston. That spark ignited something inside her, and within a few months Pat began to remember what had been done to her. She made an appointment to share these memories with her pastor.

"He was listening to my story and witnessing the pain I was in, the tears, the sobbing," she said. "There was a sense of relief of being able to reveal what happened to me to the appropriate levels of our Church."

---

[10] *Denver Catholic*, "'Forgiveness is a decision': Abuse survivor shares journey of healing and faith," by Moira Cullings, November 27, 2018.

Pat said her pastor "stood in the gap. He took all of my anger and my venom. I was free to scream and yell and curse, curse the man who did this to me. I went to reconciliation over and over and over, trying to deal with the murderous anger that I had inside of me."

Dr. Christina Lynch, director of psychological services at St. John Vianney Theological Seminary in Denver, told the *Denver Catholic* that this step is essential for the healing of abuse victims. "We all need to talk about traumatic experiences rather than just bury them where they continue to live and fester and manifest in destructive ways," she said. "Toxic memories need to be integrated into the fabric of our lives, rather than hidden away or buried."

Pat's pastor also sent her to talk to a priest who was handling abuse allegations for the archdiocese. That priest arranged for her complaint to be brought to the California diocese where the abuse had occurred, and he helped her get help with the cost of the care she required as a result of the abuse.

The fact that her pastor and a diocesan official had treated her with respect and had taken action on her behalf improved Pat's fragile relationship with the Church.

"It didn't come back from my abuser, but it came back from the larger system of which my abuser was part. It set me on a road to healing and to understanding that our Church has a lot of problems. But our Church is still the true Church of Jesus Christ."

Although the pain of the abuse and its lasting effects have not gone away, Pat said, she eventually realized that it was necessary for her to forgive her abuser: "I did not want to live the rest of my life in this angry, bitter space.

I was hurting myself, I was hurting my family members, my children. I was not a happy person."

Applying a suggestion she heard while on retreat, she pictured her abuser's face while saying the Lord's Prayer.

"The day that I prayed that prayer and his entire face became in focus for me was the day it was finished," she said. "I laid it down."

REFLECTION

While Jesus reminds us that forgiveness is intrinsic to mercy, and that we are called to forgive those who have sinned against us, it does not mean that we minimize, deny, or excuse the behavior of abusers and those who have protected them, or the damage they have caused. It does not mean that we dismiss the demand for justice, including criminal and ecclesiastical penalties. And it does not mean that we abandon the call to reform the structures of the Church that have permitted and even abetted crimes against innocent people.

We come to forgiveness by attending to and acknowledging the depth of the injury and the experience of being affected by another's sin. Forgiveness is both grace and choice; it is an ongoing process requiring prayer and careful attention to one's heart. It is in the grace of forgiveness that we find the measure of our courage to remain faithful and alive to God, to ourselves, and to one another. It is in choosing to forgive that we are freed from the frenzy of violence that would otherwise engulf us. It is here that we claim our power as participants in the ongoing healing and reformation of our Church.

Forgiving does not mean denying or suppressing our feelings, as Dr. Lynch explained. Because trauma elicits a barrage of feelings, it is imperative to recognize and respond to them. Our anger and hurt about the sexual abuse committed by clergy is about something holy: a child of God has been violated and betrayed, and the Church of God has been deeply wounded. Our anger, and all the complex feelings surrounding these crimes can lead us to action that will protect people from abuse, call offenders to account, and heal ourselves and our Church.

In the context of the abuse of a child by a trusted adult, forgiveness may seem like a radical idea. And it is, precisely, the radical idea that Jesus preached, as we read time and again in the pages of the Gospels:

- the parable of the father who instantly forgives the son who has wasted the family's wealth[11];

- the Lord's response that Peter must forgive an offending "member of the church," not seven times but seventy-seven times[12];

- the beatitude "Blessed are the merciful, for they will receive mercy"[13];

- the exhortation to "Go and learn what this means, 'I desire mercy, not sacrifice.' For I have come to call not the righteous but sinners"; [14]

- the challenge in the prayer Jesus taught us: "forgive us our debts, as we also have forgiven our debtors."[15]

And, as Jesus taught, so did he live. When a woman accused of adultery was brought before him, for instance, he did not condone her behavior, but he still opted for mercy[16]. When a paralyzed man was brought to him for healing, Jesus first forgave the man's sins—without being asked.[17] And, in the ultimate example, Jesus, while dying on the cross, prayed for forgiveness for those who were killing him.[18]

---

[11] Luke 15:11-32

[12] Matthew 18:21-22

[13] Matthew 5:7

[14] Matthew 9:13

[15] Matthew 6:12

[16] John:8:1-11

[17] Matthew 9:1-8

[18] Luke 23:34

Confronted with sexual abuse of children, the crimes and the coverup, many Catholics may need time before arriving at forgiveness. It's natural to need the time to work through emotions and weigh the crimes committed by individuals in the Church against what we believe as members of the Church.

We Catholics believe in God's mercy. We hear about it again and again in the Scriptures, and we profess it again and again in our liturgy and prayer. We also believe, because Jesus told us so in so many words, that we must extend mercy to each other. And by being merciful to others, we are merciful to ourselves, laying down a burden of resentment so that we may move more easily toward a better future.

SHARE

Take a few minutes of silence to reflect on the following. Then share your responses.

1. Why do you think Pat felt it necessary to forgive her abuser?
    How do you think her forgiveness helped her and her family?

_____

_____

_____

_____

2. Can you describe a time when you were forgiven? What was that like for you?

_____

_____

_____

_____

THE WORD OF GOD

Reader: A reading from St. Paul's Letter to the Colossians (3:12-17).

As God's chosen ones, holy and beloved, clothe yourselves with compassion, kindness, humility, meekness, and patience. Bear with one another and, if anyone has a complaint against another, forgive each other; just as the Lord has forgiven you, so you also must forgive. Above all, clothe yourselves with love, which binds everything together in perfect harmony. And let the peace of Christ rule in your hearts, to which indeed you were called in the one body. And be thankful. Let the word of Christ dwell in you richly; teach and admonish one another in all wisdom; and with gratitude in your hearts sing psalms, hymns, and spiritual songs to God. And whatever you do, in word or deed, do everything in the name of the Lord Jesus, giving thanks to God the Father through him.

The Word of the Lord.

All: Thanks be to God.

SHARE

Take a few moments to reflect on the following questions. Then share your responses:

1. How do St. Paul's words to the Colossian community challenge you?

_____

_____

_____

2. Describe a time when you struggled to make the choice to forgive someone.

_____

_____

_____

_____

REFLECTION

The sexual-abuse scandal evokes the question, what do we Catholics believe that will keep us together despite the storm around us? The answer revolves around Paul's message to the Colossians—the unity, the mutual dependence, the intimacy with God and each other that we share in the Eucharist and, by extension, in the other sacraments.

We believe in the sacramental life, from baptism to death, a life in which we touch God through physical signs and receive the Holy Spirit in our open hearts.

We believe that Christ is present in the Eucharist—not symbolically, but in his real Presence; in his Word proclaimed in the assembly; and in the assembly itself.

We believe that the sacraments unite us to Christ, to each other, and to all the celebrated and anonymous saints who came before us and now live with God.

We believe that in baptism, God calls each of us by name into community, demonstrating God's care for us and the unique gifts each of us brings to the Church.

We believe that in baptism, we receive the Holy Spirit; that this is real and not a figure of speech, and that the Spirit empowers us to be witnesses to the Gospel "out there" in the world.

We believe that we have been commissioned by Christ, as a community, to carry on his ministry of charity, mercy, and justice.

We believe that, because of this unity, we all have roles in healing the institution of the Church when it is broken.

We believe that Christ is with us until the end of time. We need to pray about this great gift and celebrate together as a community of faith. This helps us move forward together.

We believe that while those entrusted with care of the Church may fail and even commit a crime, the Church itself, as Jesus promised[19], will prevail against "the powers of death." If we believe all these things, we can say with Pat, whose story we read in this session, that our Church "has a lot of problems," but our Church is still the Church of Jesus Christ.

With that in mind, we can take Paul as our example. He was sometimes exasperated by the behavior of people in the early Christian communities. But he did not respond to those problems by giving up on building the Church. Instead, Paul sought to correct what had gone wrong as he continued his mission.

Because of what we believe, we can emulate Paul, refuse to be discouraged, and play our parts in making a better future for our Church.

---

[19] Matthew 16:18

SHARE

Take a few moments of silence to reflect on one or more of the following questions. Then share your responses:

1. Which statements of belief, above, most inspire you?

_____

_____

_____

_____

2. What do you do to keep from being discouraged?

_____

_____

_____

_____

3. In what ways do you speak up if you feel you can contribute to building up your parish or rebuilding the Church? If you have not spoken up before, do you feel more able to speak up now? How can you begin?

_____

_____

_____

_____

ACT

In this session, we have affirmed that because of our faith in Christ, we are called to live as Christ. How does this inspire you to act? Here are some examples:

1. Jot down what keeps you from being discouraged; note the beliefs for which you are most grateful.

2. Read about the journey to healing in "Onward" at the back of this book.

3. Pray and/or fast for the Church—the victim-survivors of abuse and their families, the offenders, and the bishops and others who covered up the abuse. Pray the Apostles Creed slowly and ask God to affirm your belief in the tenets of our Catholic faith.

4. Reach out to someone you know who is in need of forgiveness or mercy.

5. Go to pages.renewintl.org/healing-our-church-resources-page and read one of the articles related to this session of *Healing Our Church*.

PRAY

A PRAYER FOR THE HEALING OF OUR CHURCH

Pray together:

Good and gracious God,
We ask for healing for our wounded Church
and a way forward through this time of despair.

We cry out to you for healing for the victims of abuse
and for their families.
We cry out to you for healing for the lay faithful.
We cry out to you for healing for our clergy.

Grant our bishops the courage and wisdom
to work with the laity for the transformation of our Church.

Embrace your people with your compassionate mercy,
and restore our trust in the Church and its ministers.

Give us hope that the Church will be reformed by your grace
working in and through us.

May Jesus, the compassion and power of God,
draw us to himself in Word and Sacrament and send us forth
strengthened in faith to share his love with the world.

We ask this in the name of Jesus and through the power of the Holy Spirt,
one God for ever and ever. Amen.

LOOKING AHEAD

Prepare for the next session by reading Luke 24:13-35.

A Way Forward

FOCUS

The sexual-abuse scandal is a turning point for the Church, a renewed call to discipleship for all of her members.

PRAY

Song Suggestion: "The Lord Is My Hope," M.D. Ridge
© 1989, M.D. Ridge. Published by OCP. All rights reserved. Used with permission.
(To download, visit www.ocp.org/renew-music*)*

REFRAIN
The Lord is my hope and my glory.
The Lord is the song that I sing:
so tender and loving a shepherd,
so rooted in justice a king.
When shadow confuses my vision,
When sorrow lays claim to my heart,
God is my refuge, my rock and my shield.
I will rely on the Lord.

Pray together:

Lord, as we walk on the journey of life,
we know that you are our constant companion.
Just as you were present to the disciples of Emmaus
and their eyes were opened,
we know you are present on our journey with all
the ups and downs of life.
When we are shaken, give us hope.
When we are discouraged, lift our spirits.
When we are doubtful, enlighten our minds.
Help us to recognize you this day and every day
as we break the bread of life and share the cup of salvation.
Help us to follow your example and to listen with care
and compassion to those in pain.
Give us the wisdom to respond as Jesus would.
Renew and restore our Church,
revive our faith and give us a renewed determination
and commitment to be your disciples in our wounded Church and world.
We ask this in the name of the Father, the Son and Holy Spirit. Amen.

© RENEW International

A SURVIVOR'S STORY

Those who have been sexually abused by Catholic clergy and abandoned by some church leaders who engaged in coverup, are not the only victim-survivors of those crimes. Catholic women and men who were not directly affected by the abuse, but whose relationship with the Church has been shaken by it, are also among the survivors. An example is Mayra E. Flores, safe-environment coordinator for the Archdiocese of Chicago.

Mayra has worked for the archdiocese since 1983. In 1992, at the direction of Cardinal Joseph Bernardin, who was then archbishop of

Chicago, she and another staff member established the first diocesan office in the country dedicated to assisting victims of clergy abuse. In her present role, she oversees training of Virtus facilitators in the archdiocese: Virtus[20] training makes participants aware of the signs of sexual abuse of children, the methods and means by which offenders commit abuse, and steps that can help prevent it.

The fact that Mayra was part of the structure of the Church does not mean that it has been easy for her to continue in this work:

"There were times I doubted myself," she has written.[21] "I struggled to reconcile the conflict between my experience with the Church which had helped to form my faith and with the Church that victims-survivors said was responsible for their sexual abuse, their loss of relationships with beloved family members and, for some, their loss of a relationship with God.

"But my feelings gave way to determination. I was determined and committed to do what I could for every victim-survivor I met. It was important they knew I was humbled and honored to walk with them in their healing journey."

Mayra has written that she has been encouraged by the steps the archdiocese has taken to address this issue: "We are no longer meeting requirements as a response to a crisis. This is Church ministry to protect and heal."

---

[20] https://www.virtusonline.org/virtus/

[21] https://thehealingvoices.wordpress.com/2018/07/23/opening-the-door/

REFLECTION

Mayra, a lay person, is carrying out her part of that ministry in an official capacity. While the kind of work she does has been brought into sharp focus by the recurring waves of publicity about sexual abuse by clergy, it is not a show-window display that can be dismantled when something else captures our attention. The need to care for victims, to create a safe environment for young people, to prevent further instances of abuse—the need will never go away.

The steps that are being taken now in response to the abuse and the coverups are not designed to get us past this moment so that we can move on to something else. No, as the popular spiritual writer Fr. Ronald Rolheiser, OMI, has declared, "Carrying this crisis is now our primary ministry and not a distraction to our ministry."[22] Although most of us do not have formal roles in the Church, nevertheless, by virtue of our baptism, each of us shares in that primary ministry.

SHARE

Take a few moments of silence to reflect on the following questions. Then share your responses.

1. Has your relationship with the Church been shaken as a result of this scandal? In what way?

_____

_____

_____

_____

[22] http://ronrolheiser.com/me/uploads/2014/02/scandal.pdf

2. How has the sharing and support from your small group given you hope and helped you to find a way forward?

_____

_____

_____

_____

THE WORD OF GOD

Reader: A reading from the holy Gospel according to Luke (24:13-35)

Now on that same day two of them were going to a village called Emmaus, about seven miles from Jerusalem, and talking with each other about all these things that had happened. While they were talking and discussing, Jesus himself came near and went with them, but their eyes were kept from recognizing him. And he said to them, "What are you discussing with each other while you walk along?"

They stood still, looking sad. Then one of them, whose name was Cleopas, answered him, "Are you the only stranger in Jerusalem who does not know the things that have taken place there in these days?" He asked them, "What things?" They replied, "The things about Jesus of Nazareth, who was a prophet mighty in deed and word before God and all the people, and how our chief priests and leaders handed him over to be condemned to death and crucified him. But we had hoped that he was the one to redeem Israel. Yes, and besides all this, it is now the third day since these things took place. Moreover, some women of our group astounded us. They were at the tomb early this morning, and when they did not find his body there, they came back and told us that they had indeed seen a vision of angels who said that he was alive. Some of those who were with us went to the tomb and found it just as the women had said; but they did not see him."

Then he said to them, "Oh, how foolish you are, and how slow of heart to believe all that the prophets have declared! Was it not necessary that the Messiah should suffer these things and then enter into his glory?" Then beginning with Moses and all the prophets, he interpreted to them the things about himself in all the scriptures.

As they came near the village to which they were going, he walked ahead as if he were going on. But they urged him strongly, saying, "Stay with us, because it is almost evening and the day is now nearly over." So he went in to stay with them. When he was at the table with them, he took bread, blessed and broke it, and gave it to them. Then their eyes were opened, and they recognized him; and he vanished from their sight. They said to each other, "Were not our hearts burning within us while he was talking to us on the road, while he was opening the scriptures to us?"

That same hour they got up and returned to Jerusalem; and they found the eleven and their companions gathered together. They were saying, "The Lord has risen indeed, and he has appeared to Simon!" Then they told what had happened on the road, and how he had been made known to them in the breaking of the bread.

The Gospel of the Lord.

All: Praise to you, Lord Jesus Christ.

SHARE

Take a few moments of silence to reflect on the following questions. Then share your responses:

1. How does this Scripture passage speak to you about the theme of our final session, *A Way Forward*?

_____

_____

_____

_____

2. In what way are you like the disciples on the road to Emmaus?

_____

_____

_____

_____

REFLECTION

In one respect, the two travelers in this Gospel passage knew where they were going. Luke is explicit about that: they were going to a village named Emmaus. But in another respect, they were wandering aimlessly. The prophet in whom they had put their hopes had been betrayed and killed, and his body was missing from the tomb. They got their bearings again only when they recognized that Jesus was indeed the promised Messiah, that he had overcome death and was living among them, and that they and he were united in the Eucharist. With their faith revived, they went back to Jerusalem, back to discipleship!

The image of the journey in this passage is appropriate. There is a temptation whenever an astounding example of human weakness occurs to yearn, as did the disciples on the road to Emmaus, for some former era in which we were free of such worries. But no such time has existed in the life of the Church. There may have been periods of greater ignorance or greater silence, but the Church from the beginning has been a community of wheat and weeds, saints and sinners—among the clergy and among the laity; in fact, it has always been central to the Church's ministry to guide sinners on the way to greater holiness. As Jesus reminded the scribes, "Those who are well have no need of a physician, but those who are sick; I have come to call not the righteous but sinners."[23] This isn't an occasion for looking back to some imagined golden age; it is an occasion for us, as a Church, to find a way forward toward a better future.

That means all of us. We share with Cleopas and his companion both intimacy with Christ in the Eucharist and the call to be his witnesses, to be his comforting and challenging voice and his healing hands in the world. In this moment in the life of the Church, we have an opportunity to fulfill that vocation by doing our part in what Father Rolheiser called "our primary ministry." And it is an opportunity rather than a burden.

This situation in which so many crimes and so much malfeasance has been exposed to the light is frequently called a "crisis." That word is derived from a nearly identical Greek word that means the turning point in the progress of a disease—the decisive moment at which the malady can start to dissipate or grow worse. This turning point in the life of the Church is an opportunity for all of us to do what we can to heal those who have been harmed, reassure those who are innocent, and contribute to an environment in which sexual abuse is unlikely to occur and, if it does, cannot be hidden.

---

[23] Mark 2:17

In order to do our part in finding the way forward, we must recall again that we are the Church, all of us—the faith-filled laity, women and men in religious life, deacons, priests, and bishops. That means that we lay people are partners with those who are ordained or consecrated in building the Church's future, not because we share responsibility for the wrongs that have been done, but rather because those wrongs have harmed all of us, the Church. As St. Paul pointed out in his analogy of the parts of the human body, none of us is more or less important in this mission. "The eye cannot say to the hand, 'I have no need of you,' nor again the head to the feet, 'I have no need of you.'"[24]

As indispensable members of the Church, we can do many things to help each other and the whole Body of Christ embark on the way forward:

- Pray, pray always, for those who have been subject to abuse, for the families of victims, for faithful clergy, and for the priests who committed these crimes and the bishops who protected them.

- Remain fully engaged in the sacramental life of the Church, experiencing the inexhaustible mercy of God and the unity Jesus prayed for.

- Know what your diocese and your parish have done to protect children from abuse. Ask questions; make suggestions.

- Take advantage of opportunities to learn how to recognize child abuse, wherever it occurs.

- Help your children to recognize signs of abusive behavior and encourage them to reveal it immediately.

- Speak up to competent authorities if you suspect someone is being abused.

---

[24] 1 Corinthians 12:21

- Inform yourself about lay movements inside and outside the Church that are designed to assist victims and create safe environments. Consider what part you might play in these movements.

- Be proactive in letting your diocese and parish know that you will accept nothing less than zero tolerance of sexual abuse and immediate, correct response to such behavior.

- Tell your pastor that you are ready to help him assure that your parish is a safe place for children.

- Sign up for the Virtus training mentioned in the Survivor's Story and volunteer to assist in any program at your parish that involves children.

- Offer your expertise—if you are a counselor or mental health professional, for example—wherever it may be helpful in assisting victims or the Church.

- Reassure and support clergy, clearly the majority in the Church, who faithfully carry out their ministries. Let your pastor know he is not alone with the demands of his ministry.

If the sexual-abuse scandal has left us discouraged and adrift, like Cleopas and his friend, our recourse, like theirs, is in the Paschal Mystery that is central to our Catholic faith: Jesus suffered and died, but then overcame both death and sin. That is the heart of our faith, that in Jesus life emerges from death. This mystery describes what happened to the historic Jesus, of course, but it also describes the life of every Catholic Christian who believes that sin gives way to penance and forgiveness, that discouragement gives way to hope. Ours is an optimistic faith. We witness to the resurrection of Jesus not by collapsing under the weight of this scandal in the Church but by acknowledging it, praying and working to eradicate it, and continuing together in the Church's mission of reconciliation, charity, and justice.

"The Church" has been excoriated for the sins that have been committed and hidden, and it will be the focus of more criticism as more records are made public and more investigations undertaken in dioceses around the country. But we know that while that condemnation might be justly directed at the institution, its structures and systems, the Church that is the Body of Christ, all of us, has not abandoned the mission Jesus gave it to "teach all nations," heal the sick, feed the poor, and comfort the forsaken. We condemn the scandal; we face it and deal with it; but we do not let it distract us from our baptismal mission. The Church can move forward from this dark time, because we are the Church, "a people born to rise and rise again."[25]

The conclusion of these six sessions of *Healing Our Church* is not an end but a beginning, for us personally and for the Church. We hear amid the troubles that have harmed the innocent and scandalized the Church a renewed call to discipleship. May we respond not by giving in to discouragement but by walking the way forward together as a family of faith.

SHARE

Take a few moments of silence to reflect on one or more of the following points. Then share your responses.

1. Has there been a crisis in your life that became a turning point that helped you grow and become a better person and disciple of Jesus?

_____

_____

_____

_____

[25] From "In This Day, O God," © 1977 The Benedictine Foundation of the State of Vermont, Inc.

2. How can this crisis be a turning point for the Church to become holier and more responsive to the needs of the world? As an indispensable member of the Church, what can you do to help find a way forward for each other, for your parish?

_____

_____

_____

_____

ACT

In this session, we have reflected on the sexual-abuse crisis as a renewed call to discipleship for the Church and all her members. How does this inspire you to act? Here are some examples in addition to those already mentioned in this session:

1. Commit to attending the *Healing Our Church* evening of prayer and reflection with all the groups in your parish.

2. Fill out the reflection sheet at the end of this session and share some of your insights at the evening of prayer and reflection.

3. Commit to praying RENEW's "Healing for Our Church" prayer once a week.

4. Send a note to your pastor or to another priest you know, telling him how much you appreciate him and that you are praying for him.

5. Take an active role in your parish by volunteering in some capacity.

6. Commit to meet again as a small group with one of RENEW's small-group resources. See pages 93-96.

7. A committee at St. Vincent de Paul Parish in Baltimore has compiled a list of primary-source documents designed to contribute to a better understanding of the factors that led to the sexual-abuse scandal and possible steps forward.[26] Consider recommending that your parish provide such a resource; volunteer to help compile it.

8. Go to pages.renewintl.org/healing-our-church-resources-page and read one of the articles related to this session of *Healing Our Church*.

SENDING-FORTH PRAYER

Leader: As we complete the final session of *Healing Our Church*, we thank God for our time together and ask God to lead us to a way forward as wounded healers to our Church and world.

Reader: A reading from Henri Nouwen's *The Wounded Healer*:[27]

"We all are wounded people, whether physically, emotionally, mentally, or spiritually. The main question is not, 'How can we hide our wounds?' so we don't have to be embarrassed, but, 'How can we put our woundedness into the service of others?' When our wounds cease to be a source of shame, and become a source of healing, we have become wounded healers."

Take a few moments for quiet reflection.

---

[26] http://www.stvchurch.org/2018/09/07/church-reform-primary-source-documents/

[27] Henri Nouwen, op. cit.

Leader: For whom and what do you pray tonight? Our response is "Lord, hear our prayer."

Group members share their intentions.

Leader: Let us pray in the words our Savior taught us.

The group prays the Lord's Prayer together.

Leader: Let us pray.

A PRAYER FOR THE HEALING OF OUR CHURCH

The group prays:

Good and gracious God,
We ask for healing for our wounded Church
and a way forward through this time of despair.

We cry out to you for healing for the victims of abuse
and for their families.
We cry out to you for healing for the lay faithful.
We cry out to you for healing for our clergy.

Grant our bishops the courage and wisdom
to work with the laity for the transformation of our Church.

Embrace your people with your compassionate mercy,
and restore our trust in the Church and its ministers.

Give us hope that the Church will be reformed by your grace
working in and through us.

May Jesus, the compassion and power of God,
draw us to himself in Word and Sacrament and send us forth
strengthened in faith to share his love with the world.

We ask this in the name of Jesus and through the power of the Holy Spirt,
one God for ever and ever. Amen.

CLOSING RITE

Leader:　　Blessed be the name of the Lord.
Response:　Now and forever.

Leader:　　Our help is in the name of the Lord.
Response:　Who made heaven and earth.

Leader:　　May almighty God bless us, in the name of the Father,
　　　　　　　the Son, and the Holy Spirit.
Response:　Amen.

Leader:　　Go forth and announce the Gospel of the Lord.
Response:　Thanks be to God.

Leader:　　Go in peace, glorifying the Lord by your life.
Response:　Thanks be to God.

Leader:　　Go in peace, healing our wounded Church.
Response:　Thanks be to God.

Leader:　　Let us exchange with one another a sign of peace.
Response:　Amen.

REVIEW AND REFLECT

After completing these sessions, parishes may choose to hold a Gathering of Prayer and Reflection during which you may share some of your thoughts from this page.

1. What were your feelings coming into this group and this topic? How have your feelings changed as a result of *Healing Our Church*?

   Felt like trying to understand from others standpoints what could help heal my feelings

2. What were your key learnings?

   Everyone makes mistakes but those who hide them make it worse for all of us.

3. Which action steps did you take that had the most impact?

   Coming to this session has shed a lot of different perspective on these incidents good and bad.

4. What questions do you still have?

   How many steps will be taken to prevent a scandal like this from happening again.

5. Other thoughts:

   Hope by learning from this we can move forward and take steps so this may never happen again.

ONWARD

We hope that *Healing Our Church* has been an experience of grace and blessing for all who have participated in this invitation to engage in prayer, reflection, and action. These sessions from RENEW International present a spiritually rich and psychologically sound means of tending to the pain of God's people amid the sexual-abuse scandal in the hope that we might not become captive to the searing anguish and deep disappointment of it all.

The journey to healing takes time. Crisis and trauma tear at the hearts of all whose needs for safety, truth, and trust have been tattered, if not shattered. The present scandal in the Church may also reawaken earlier experiences of crisis and trauma in our lives, because "here and now" often triggers our experience of "there and then." Such awareness, while perhaps provoking some initial anxiety, might be an invitation to consider a healing process (such as psychotherapy, counseling, spiritual direction, or music/art therapy) to promote wholeness and wellness in mind, body, and spirit.

As a people of faith who "know that all things work together for good for those who love God,"[28] we need not fear or shut down any experience of our innermost being, but rather face it, name it, process it, and pray it, in trust of the Spirit whose healing, life-giving, and renewing energy is alive within us and amongst us. Because we believe that God is with us, we can also trust that God will lead us to personal and communal awareness of how best to continue the journey that deepens healing for each one and everyone. Your experience of the crisis within our Church, along with all that it stirs within you, will undoubtedly continue to unfold as allegations

---

[28] Romans 8:28

and investigations develop throughout the country. May you resolve to stay attentive and follow the Spirit's lead to how you are being called to continue your healing journey.

God who has begun this healing work in us will bring it to completion in God's time. In the meantime, the grace and power of this Spirit is unleashed when we acknowledge reality and we are "speaking the truth in love."[29] Indeed, it is our vulnerability and openness to the inspiration of the Holy Spirit that empowers us to listen to and speak from the depths of our hearts, while also being open to our sisters and brothers as they listen to and speak from their own hearts.

The God in whose image we are created calls us each by name into communion with God, with community, and with one another. When we were baptized into God's abundant life, the Spirit was poured into our hearts. The love of God's Spirit animates our compassion, forgiveness, and healing; the light of God's Spirit inspires our wisdom, truth, and insight. May God continue to empower us to choose "to keep on keeping on"—walking, talking, working, praying, and discerning our way into the peace of Christ, whose plentiful love tends and heals our wounds and brings us to fullness of life.

This program has been designed as one part of a multi-faceted process to foster healing for both the community of the Church and for persons within it whose lives have been painfully impacted by the abuse and the scandal. While the completion of these six sessions marks the conclusion of this specific program, it is essential to note that the journey to healing is ongoing and, in many ways, a lifelong process. Your continued commitment to attentive and compassionate listening, to honest and

---

[29] Ephesians 4:15

courageous conversation, to faith-filled and humble prayer, and to bold and prophetic action will create even more space, within your own soul and within the heart of the Church, for the healing that is God's blessing and our longing.

"Now to him who by the power at work within us is able to accomplish abundantly far more than all we can ask or imagine, to him be glory in the church and in Christ Jesus to all generations, forever and ever." Amen. (Ephesians 3:20).

Rev. John Collins, C.Ss.R., LCSW

Father Collins is a counselor/psychotherapist, a spiritual director, and a member of the staff at St. Alfonso Retreat House, Long Branch, New Jersey.

Victim Assistance Coordinators

If you or someone in your care has been the victim of sexual abuse by a priest, deacon, or individual representing the Catholic Church in a diocese or eparchy in the United States, there are several things you can do:

- Contact the appropriate law-enforcement agency to file a report and to determine if the incident falls within the statute of limitations in the jurisdiction in which the offense occurred.
- Contact local child-protection agencies, a private attorney, or a support group.
- Contact the victim assistance coordinator in your diocese. This is particularly important for help, healing, and response from the diocese.

You can find the victim assistance coordinator for your diocese by calling the diocesan center, visiting the diocese's website, or visiting http://usccb.org/issues-and-action/child-and-youth-protection/victim-assistance-coordinators.cfm

Hotlines

- National Sexual Assault Telephone Hotline: 1-800-656-4673
  https://www.rainn.org/
- National Child Abuse Hotline:1-800-422-4453
  https://www.childhelp.org/

Resources Online

For articles and other information related to each session of this book, visit pages.renewintl.org/healing-our-church-resources-page. After each session, read one of the related articles for more background and context.

About RENEW International

The RENEW process, both parish-based and diocese-wide, was developed and implemented in the Archdiocese of Newark, New Jersey. Its success there led other dioceses to bring RENEW to their people in over 160 dioceses in the United States and 24 countries.

Over more than four decades, RENEW International has grown from its original single RENEW process. Materials and training have been inculturated and made available in more than 40 languages. We have added specific pastoral outreach to campuses and to young adults in their 20s and 30s. We have incorporated prison ministry and provided resources for the visually impaired.

The core of all these processes remains the same: to help people become better hearers and doers of the Word of God. We do this by encouraging and supporting the formation of small communities that gather prayerfully to reflect on and share the Word of God, to make better connections between faith and life, and to live their faith more concretely in family, work, and community life.

As a not-for-profit organization, we sustain our pastoral outreach in part from the sales of our publications and resources and stipends for services we provide to parishes and dioceses. However, our priority is always to serve all parishes that desire to renew their faith and build the Church, regardless of their economic situation. We have been able to fulfill this mission not only in the inner-city and rural areas of the United States, but also in the developing world, especially Latin America and Africa, thanks to donations and charitable funding.

As you meet in your small group, we invite you to take a few moments to imagine the great invisible network of others, here in the United States and on other continents. They gather, as you do, in small Christian communities, around the Word of God present in the Scripture, striving to hear and act upon that Word. Keep them in your prayer: a prayer of thanksgiving for the many graces we have experienced; a prayer that the Holy Spirit will guide all of us as we strive together to Heal Our Church.

The Structure and Flow of a Session

A faith-sharing session typically lasts about 90 minutes. The following outline for your weekly small-group meeting suggests how your time might be allocated in order to keep the group moving smoothly from one element to the next. The time frame described here is based on the assumption that participants have read the session beforehand and considered their responses to the sharing questions, making notes in the spaces provided. Of course, the group leader may adjust the timing according to the dynamics of a particular session.

More detailed suggestions for the leader are included in *Essentials for Small Group Leaders* and *Leading Prayer in Small Groups*, both available from RENEW International. For details, visit www.renewintl.org.

Introductions (First session only) 5 minutes
An opportunity to get acquainted is important. People share most easily when they feel comfortable and accepted in a group.

Focus • 1 minute
Read the focus to call to mind the central theme of the session.

Opening Song • 3-4 minutes
Play a song recommended for the session or a song of your own choosing.

Opening Prayer • 5 minutes
A few moments of silence should precede the prayer, which is always at the heart of gatherings of Christians.

A Survivor's Story and Reflection • 20 minutes

Members of the group take a few minutes to review the Survivor's Story and the Reflection based on it, or members of the group could read the text aloud. Then those who wish may share their responses to the questions.

The Word of God • 20 minutes

A member of the group reads the scripture passage aloud. After a few moments of silent reflection, members may respond to the question following the passage.

Reflection 2 • 20 minutes

Members of the group take a few minutes to review the Reflection, or members of the group could read the text aloud. Then those who wish may share their responses to the questions.

Act • 10 minutes

Members of the group discuss the suggested actions listed in the session and any actions the session may have inspired in them.

Closing Prayer • 5 minutes

ARISE Together in Christ

Healing our Church is a beginning, not an end. While it will provide a path for working through the immediate issues, we need to look beyond to what is possible for our Church. *ARISE Together in Christ* is a three-year, parish-centered process of spiritual renewal and evangelization that enables people to deepen their faith, develop a closer relationship with Christ, grow in community, and reach out in service to others. It emphasizes people living in good relationship with one another, as they make concrete applications of the Gospel to their life situations. *ARISE Together in Christ* is a total renewal experience for the parish, spiritually transforming people through small Christian communities, special parish activities, reflections for families with teens and children, and Christian social action. There are five six-week seasons:

- *Season One:* **Encountering Christ Today**
- *Season Two:* **Change Our Hearts**
- *Season Three:* **In the Footsteps of Christ**
- *Season Four:* **New Heart, New Spirit**
- *Season Five:* **We Are the Good News!**

A Complete Integrated Process

For a complete, integrated experience of *ARISE Together in Christ*, RENEW International recommends using the resources as part of a comprehensive diocese-wide, parish-based process that includes training for leaders, pastoral support and online tools and materials.

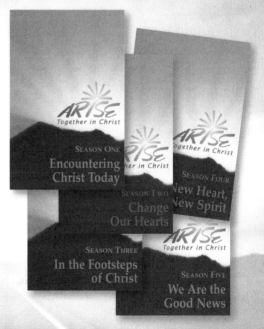

ARISE Together in Christ small-group materials appear in English, Spanish, Portuguese, Haitian Creole, Chinese and Vietnamese.

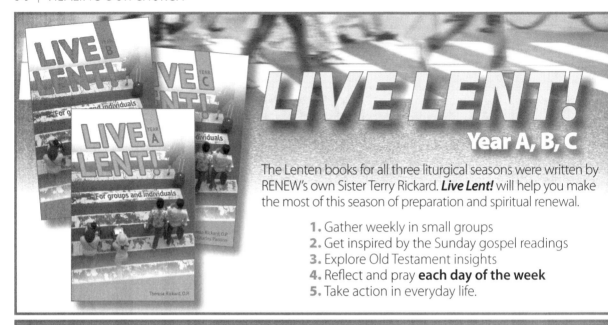

LIVE LENT!

Year A, B, C

The Lenten books for all three liturgical seasons were written by RENEW's own Sister Terry Rickard. **Live Lent!** will help you make the most of this season of preparation and spiritual renewal.

1. Gather weekly in small groups
2. Get inspired by the Sunday gospel readings
3. Explore Old Testament insights
4. Reflect and pray **each day of the week**
5. Take action in everyday life.

ADVENT AWAKENINGS

Advent is a time of spiritual anticipation amidst the often distracting preparations for Christmas. Stay focused on the significance of this season with **Advent Awakenings**, a four-session faith-sharing experience grounded in the Sunday gospel readings.

The **Advent Awakenings** series is based on the three-year cycle of the **Lectionary**. Each book contains four sessions corresponding with the four Sundays of Advent and presents themes drawn from the Sunday gospel readings, plus enriching devotions for family use. Appropriate for seasonal groups, small Christian communities, and individual reflection and prayer.

- *Year B: **Take the Time:*** Encourages participants to prepare for Jesus' coming by setting aside everyday busyness and becoming more deeply aware of God's beckoning.

- *Year A: **Trust the Lord:*** Urges participants to have confidence that God's challenging call is the true way to prepare for union with Christ.

- *Year C: **Say Yes to God:*** Prompts participants to accept the invitation of Jesus' coming by reflecting on how to be more open to his presence in their lives.

- Also available as an eBook!

For more information visit **www.renewintl.org/seasonal**

RENEW
Small-Group
Leader Series

Learn from the wisdom of RENEW International's three decades of experience promoting and sustaining small Christian communities. Foster spiritual renewal by empowering individuals and communities to encounter God in everyday life, deepen and share faith, and connect faith to action.

Essentials for Small Community Leaders

This book offers a comprehensive collection of pastoral insights and practical suggestions to help small-community leaders guide their groups in a way that nourishes spiritual growth. Culled from RENEW International's almost four decades of experience in pioneering and promoting small Christian communities, this book overflows with simple but effective ideas and strategies that will enhance the way these groups reflect on and respond to the Gospel.

- Also available as an eBook!
- Disponible en español: *Sembradores de semillas*

Leading Prayer in Small Groups

Have you ever been asked to lead prayer for your church group, council, or committee? RENEW International has developed a helpful new resource called **Leading Prayer in Small Groups** to encourage you in leading fruitful group prayer experiences with confidence. **Leading Prayer in Small Groups** emphasizes the importance of group prayer for church groups of every kind and provides insight into why we pray. It also explains the role, qualities, and duties of a leader of prayer. Readers are guided through the stages of preparing group prayer and the process of effectively leading prayer for a group.

For more information visit **www.renewintl.org/leaders**

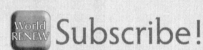
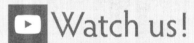

NOTES

NOTES

NOTES

NOTES